THEOLOGY AND SCIENCE AT THE FRONTIERS OF KNOWLEDGE

NUMBER THREE

SCIENCE AND THEOLOGY
IN EINSTEIN'S PERSPECTIVE

THEOLOGY AND SCIENCE AT THE FRONTIERS OF KNOWLEDGE

1: T. F. Torrance, *Reality and Scientific Theology.*
2: H. P. Nebelsick, *Circles of God, Theology and Science from the Greeks to Copernicus.*
3: Iain Paul, *Science and Theology in Einstein's Perspective.*
4: Alexander Thomson, *Tradition and Authority in Science and Theology.*
5: R. G. Mitchell, *Einstein and Christ, A New Approach to the Defence of the Christian Religion.*
6: W. G. Pollard, *Transcendence and Providence, Reflections of a Physicist and Priest.*

THEOLOGY AND SCIENCE AT THE FRONTIERS OF KNOWLEDGE

GENERAL EDITOR – T. F. TORRANCE

SCIENCE AND THEOLOGY IN EINSTEIN'S PERSPECTIVE

IAIN PAUL

SCOTTISH ACADEMIC PRESS
EDINBURGH
1986

Published in association with the
Center of Theological Inquiry, Princeton
and
The Templeton Foundation Inc.
by
SCOTTISH ACADEMIC PRESS
33 Montgomery Street, Edinburgh EH7 5JX

First published 1986

ISBN 0 7073 0449 0

© Iain Paul, 1986

All rights reserved. No part of this publication may be reproduced, stored in a retrieval system, or transmitted in any form or by any means, electronic, mechanical, photocopying, recording or otherwise, without the prior permission of Scottish Academic Press Limited.

British Library Cataloguing in Publication Data

Paul, Iain
   Science and theology in Einstein's perspective.
   1. Einstein, Albert
   2. Religion and science—1946–
   I. Title
   215'.092'4   BL240

ISBN 0-7073-0449-0

Printed in Great Britain by
Clark Constable, Edinburgh and London

To
Mum and Dad Russell

CONTENTS

General Foreword	ix
Preface	xiii

Chapter

1.	Introduction	1
2.	Scientific Faith	8
3.	Scientific Knowledge	20
4.	Scientific Communication	36
5.	The Universe	48
6.	Universal Unity	57
7.	Universal Authority	64
8.	The Rationality of the Universe	73
9.	The Intuitive Relation	84
10.	Motivation and Community	94

GENERAL FOREWORD

A VAST shift in the perspective of human knowledge is taking place, as a unified view of the one created world presses for realisation in our understanding. The destructive dualisms and abstractions which have disintegrated form and fragmented culture are being replaced by unitary approaches to reality in which thought and experience are wedded together in every field of scientific inquiry and in every area of human life and culture. There now opens up a dynamic, open-structured universe, in which the human spirit is being liberated from its captivity in closed deterministic systems of cause and effect, and a correspondingly free and open-structured society is struggling to emerge.

The universe that is steadily being disclosed to our various sciences is found to be characterised throughout time and space by an ascending gradient of meaning in richer and higher forms of order. Instead of levels of existence and reality being explained reductionistically from below in materialistic and mechanistic terms, the lower levels are found to be explained in terms of higher, invisible, intangible levels of reality. In this perspective the divisive splits become healed, constructive syntheses emerge, being and doing become conjoined, an integration of form takes place in the sciences and the arts, the natural and the spiritual dimensions overlap, while knowledge of God and of his creation go hand in hand and bear constructively on one another.

We must now reckon with a revolutionary change in the generation of fundamental ideas. Today it is no longer philosophy but the physical and natural sciences which set the pace in human culture through their astonishing revelation of the rational structures that pervade and underly all created reality. At the same time, as our science presses its inquiries to the very boundaries of being, in macrophysical and microphysical dimensions alike, there is being brought to light a hidden traffic between theological and scientific ideas of the most far-reaching significance for both theology and science. It is in that situation where theology and science are found to have deep mutual relations, and increasingly cry out for each other, that our authors have been at work.

The different volumes in this series are intended to be geared into this fundamental change in the foundations of knowledge. They do not present 'hack' accounts of scientific trends or theological fashions, but are intended to offer inter-disciplinary and creative interpretations which will themselves share in and carry forward the new synthesis transcending the gulf in popular understanding between faith and reason, religion and life, theology and science. Of special concern is the mutual modification and cross-fertilisation between natural and theological science, and the creative integration of all human thought and culture within the universe of space and time.

What is ultimately envisaged is a reconstruction of the very foundations of modern thought and culture, similar to that which took place in the early centuries of the Christian era, when the unitary outlook of Judaeo-Christian thought transformed that of the ancient world, and made possible the eventual rise of modern empirico-theoretic science. The various books in this series are written by scientists and by theologians, and by some who are both scientists and theologians. While they differ in training, outlook, religious persuasion, and nationality, they are all passionately committed to the struggle for a unified understanding of the one created universe and the healing of our split culture. Many difficult questions are explored and discussed, and the ground needs to be cleared of often deep-rooted misconceptions, but the results are designed to be presented without technical detail or complex argumentation, so that they can have their full measure of impact upon the contemporary world.

In this book Dr. Iain Paul, who holds doctorates in both physical science and systematic theology, explores the epistemological interrelations between natural science and theology. In an earlier work, *Science, Theology and Einstein*, 1982, he turned his attention mainly upon natural science, but here he lays the stress also upon Christian theology. His aim is to offer a discussion unencumbered by technicalities which will help to dismantle inbuilt prejudices of scientists against theology and of theologians against science, by drawing out the implications of new perspectives in the structure of knowledge brought about by Albert Einstein. Science and theology are shown to have wide areas of mutual concern in their respective inquiries, but the argument is carried further to reveal that this mutual concern reaches beyond questions of formal method and research into material content and controlling ideas. With all the differences imposed by the distinctive nature of their fields, they are found to work with fundamental conceptions which can be paralleled to each other in such a way as to help scientists and theologians to understand and appreciate one another in a fresh and rather enlightening way.

Thomas F. Torrance

Edinburgh,
Advent, 1984

PREFACE

THIS short essay is an attempt to show that modern science and Christian theology are not radically opposed to each other. When Albert Einstein's twentieth century views on scientific research are compared with the fourth century theological statements of Athanasius, vast areas of mutual interest are briefly illuminated. In the light of this comparison, it becomes strikingly apparent that Einstein has set the stage for contemporary discussions of the relation of science and theology by communicating that sense of action which is scientific research.

Outlines of the similarities between scientific and Christian faith, scientific and theological knowledge, scientific and theological communication, the universe and God, universal and divine unity, universal and divine authority, the rationality of the universe and Jesus Christ, and the intuitive relation and the Holy Spirit are drawn from an Einsteinian perspective. A brief discussion of motivation and community concludes the essay.

Once modern science is apprehended in terms of the openness and realism characteristic of the theology of Athanasius and echoed in the writings of Einstein, Christians can penetrate to the hospitable reality behind the hostile appearances of modern scientific endeavours. They can place themselves in a much better position to curb anti-scientific or anti-Christian bias and to contribute to the ongoing dialogue between modern science and Christian theology.

It is hoped that the partial and inadequate views presented in this essay will be corrected and enriched by Christian thinkers and scientific researchers. It is with such tentativeness that this contribution is offered. Both scientific research and Christian theology have taught the author that even to fail in what is undoubtedly a great and exciting task is to make the path easier for the more capable who follow. While the discussion offered here has its own aim, it can be read as a sequel to *Science, Theology and Einstein*, 1982.

I should like to express my indebtedness to my patrons, the Trustees of the Center of Theological Inquiry, Princeton, and to Dr. L. Charles Willard and the staff of the Robert E. Speer Library, who made the writing of this essay so agreeably possible. My debts to the Reverend Dr. James I. McCord, Chancellor, the Center of Theological Inquiry, formerly President and Professor of Theology, Princeton Theological Seminary, and to the Very Reverend Dr. Thomas F. Torrance, Emeritus Professor of Christian Dogmatics, University of Edinburgh, for their sensitive encouragement and inexhaustible kindness cannot be adequately expressed in words. I should also like very specially to thank Jean (Mrs. Stewart) McIntyre who prepared the typescript accurately, swiftly and cheerfully.

CHAPTER 1

INTRODUCTION

THE theology of this century, like its science, is not that of the last century. Nor will it be the theology of the next century. But many people in this so-called scientific age are not content to wait for decades on the theological change. The science of today, unlike its theology, is not that of yesterday. Nor will it be the science of tomorrow. Although theology exhibits a similar character of gradual development, modern science is much more obviously and rapidly changeable than theology. Even scientists find it difficult to keep abreast of current scientific developments in areas far removed from their own researches. By contrast, the barely perceptible dynamics of modern theological concepts often leads interested scientists to doubt the value of systematic theology. Moreover, the descried immutability of theological concepts encourages some of them to regard the technical vocabulary of theology as mere camouflage to conceal contradiction, paradox and creative impotence.

Understandably, the relatively slow development of modern theology tends to frustrate the heuristically tuned scientific mind. Yet, that neither gives scientists the right to dismiss theology as a contrived system for the transference of real mysteries to the obscurity of a technical library, nor justifies the assumption that theologians have been playing Rip van Winkle for the last few centuries. In both scientific and theological thought, modification, elaboration and clarification are at work. Consequently, the same assertions made today as were made hundreds of years ago are subject to expansions or limitations of meaning which were not previously recognised. Just as no theologian could subscribe without qualification to the beliefs of Tertullian,

Athanasius, Augustine or Calvin, no scientist could embrace without reservation the beliefs of Copernicus, Galileo, Newton or Einstein. A general feature of all concepts is that their validities are always open to further elucidation, amplification or limitation by as yet undiscovered conceptions. The prevailing conceptual climate has to promote the growth of new concepts and to safeguard the validity of older ones.

Scientists seldom venture too far in their theorizing from the data of experience. But this proclivity also causes many of them to question, often involuntarily, the relevance of an apparently remote discipline like systematic theology. The latter deserves careful consideration, however, if only for the sake of science itself. To many educated citizens, for whom scientific research and technological development are distinguishable, both science and theology seem too distant from the urgencies of every day living. For them, daily life demands immediate solutions to pressing practical problems, not high performances in what appears to be sheer intellectual indulgence. Modern living is geared to the alteration of the environment and its contents as the means of the immediate increase of man's comfort and convenience. Whereas science searches for the way of the universe, the inventions and ingenuity of technology serve various definite human purposes. Modern science may perform wonders but they are not always needed, wanted or even welcomed by man. It leaves the choice between wanton exploitation and responsible stewardship to society. Consequently, when those people hear of scientists condemning theological activity as an excessive elaboration of Christian teaching, they are reminded of the leaf calling the stem green. Moreover, this instinctive identification of a profound similarity is not to be despised. In the face of it, scientists who are also Christians cannot evade their responsibilities.

Perhaps surprising to many scientists, Albert Einstein's comment on a common misreading of scientific researchers is readily applicable to a popular misrepresentation of theologians. "Those whose acquaintance with scientific research is derived chiefly from its practical results easily develop a completely false notion of men who, surrounded by a skeptical world, have shown the way to kindred spirits scattered wide through the world and the centuries."[1] The relatively low profile and population density of modern systematic theologians together with the comparatively high rate of technological innovation in modern pragmatic societies conspire to elevate the man of immediate action, even within Christianity.

The person who produces speedy results is rapidly idolised while those who concern themselves with the bases of faith are soon branded as people who think too much for their own good. It is of very little consequence to some that quick results frequently promise eventual failure in the things that really matter. In short, empathy is a luxury more often currently denied the devoted theologian than the dedicated scientist. Yet, their respective conceptual systems can only change in so far as scientists and theologians are prepared to strive long and hard to experience and to learn more. However, in spite of the disinterested or discouraging populace, numerous persons are inspired to pursue the arduous aims of scientific research and theological activity. In plain language, both subjects move interested parties to do something about them.

Modern science and systematic theology have a common concern with all that lies between the birth of the universe and the end of the world. On the one hand, science studies the text of the book of natural order. On the other hand, it reads the available charts of the landscape of scientific thought. Similarly, on the one side, systematic theology explores the contents of the sacred and inspired Scriptures. On the other side, it ponders the received doctrines as the condensed Christian reflection of generations. Scientific research stretches from the nature of the sub-nuclear particle to the structure of the universe, while systematic theology reaches from the jot and tittle of Scripture to the *Alpha* and the *Omega* of the creation. In neither case are the problems arbitrary. Always, they arise within a living context and, therefore, they exhibit a dynamic continuity.

Each discipline displays a vibrant form and a creative content developed through the centuries by the co-ordinative tension between experience and reflection. This tension characterises both activities that have much more in common than is generally appreciated.

Albeit obliquely, Einstein actually underscored the kinship of the scientist and the theologian. "Only one who has devoted his life to similar ends can have a vivid realization of what has inspired these men and given them the strength to remain true to their purpose in spite of countless failures."[2] Of course, Einstein was referring to the dedication of scientists, and his words may not be acceptable to the theological rigorist. Nevertheless, they do capture something of the spirit of theological activity.

His own researches had convinced Einstein that an immoderate emphasis on practical results is atypical of those who are intimate with the intensive demands of an exacting discipline.[3] Indeed, acutely aware of their own inadequacies, scientists and theologians know, as a rule, the ease with which they can lapse into an inflated sense of achievement. Over sixteen hundred years ago, Athanasius stated the theological case bluntly, ". . . to turn away from the Word of God, which is, and to fashion . . . one that is not, is to fall to what is nothing."[4] Seductive expediency and rampant speculation are equally blind to scientific discovery and theological inquiry. They are formidable adversaries who never retire from the intellectual arena. It takes more than idle curiosity or mild interest to stay in there with them and to strive hopefully for long-term objectives.

Theological thinking, like scientific thinking, requires what Einstein called passionate devotion.[5] A theological necessity constrains members of the Church to seek a greater apprehension of God and of his universe. Likewise, a scientific necessity is laid upon some members of society to discover a deeper understanding of nature.[6] In both cases the mandate is clearly to commit oneself fully, including all the mind, to an ever changing world which presents new problems, questions and opportunities.

The meaning and justification of scientific or theological reflection lie in the corresponding activity itself, not in previously preferred results. The awareness of scientists or of theologians is primarily of the reality which exists before and beyond the particular topic in hand. In scientific or theological thinking there is a logical manifold or reasoned coherence which results from a heuristic dynamics or exploratory propulsion.[7] By expanding a logical survey through a responsible re-ordering or re-interpretation of experience, the scientist or theologian engages in a heuristic event. This act is rationally irreversible being grounded in that reality which alone nourishes apprehension. In other words, anti-intellectualism has no legitimate place in modern science or in Christian teaching.

Neither, for that matter, has hyper-intellectualism which raises its own crop of problems. By hyper-intellectualism is meant that condition of mind which regards all forms of ignorance, except its own, as manifestations of gross inferiority. For example, a theoretical or exegetical apparatus, when wielded as a club to defend occupied territory or to display erudition, transforms discussions into disputes. Then, severely debilitating blows are inflicted on innocent observers and guilty participants alike. Instead of being intellectual ploughshares, those creations become surrogate swords in the hands of the fickle for the intimidation of the uninitiated. But the matter does not always rest there. Previously wounded by such unfortunate experiences, many people no longer set much store by modern science or by systematic theology.

Frequently, in both science and theology those who hanker after wisdom are discouraged from diagnosing internal disorder by their exposure to its painful symptoms. In many instances, the hiatus between motivation and apprehension, coupled to a lack of practical experience, goes virtually undetected. The consequent distorted presentations of data repel further interest indefinitely. The fundamental point is that the formal machinery of science or theology, if idolized, is likely to scythe the ripening aspirations of those who seek genuine illumination. Formal idolatry invariably gains ground as scientists or theologians convert the powerful potentialities of increasing apprehension to aberrant species of possession. When passionate devotion, which demands humility, gives way to wilful manipulation, faith, freedom and enthusiasm are slowly strangled. That is, the story of the tower of Babel is re-enacted daily in science and theology. Clearly, they are not as different as rock and sand. At the very minimum, their foundations and frameworks leave ample scope for similar kinds of abuse.

The following sections of this essay are not intended to supply complete answers, but rather to open up lines of thought and action which may be fruitful in the dialogue between science and theology. Surely it is better to take a faltering step forward than to stand comfortably looking backward. Some salient aspects of the similarity between science and theology are presented in the hope that others will take them into account in reaching their own conclusions. The writings of Athanasius and Albert Einstein serve as guides along the way of similarity. Reasoning by similarity does not guarantee apprehension, but when an extensive correspondence is so readily available, it seems sensible to look at it carefully. The similarity between the scientific enterprise and theological activity is now outlined with the aim of urging other Christians beyond the limitations and inadequacies of this outline to greater precision and fuller apprehension through the personal participation of interested parties. From an Einsteinian perspective, sound critical thinking becomes possible only where reliable working knowledge of the subject has been assimilated. It seems rational, therefore, to adhere in the present context to the scientific way by setting up some of the apparatus that will assist the investigations of the much more capable who follow.

NOTES

1. A. Einstein, *Ideas and Opinions*, translated by Sonja Bargmann, London: Souvenir Press, 1973, p. 247.
2. *Ibid.*

3. A. Einstein, in *Albert Einstein: Philosopher-Scientist*, edited P. A. Schilpp, New York: Tudor Publishing Company, 1951, pp. 21f.
4. P. Schaff and H. Wace, *The Nicene and Post-Nicene Fathers of the Christian Church*, Volume IV *Athanasius*, Grand Rapids: W. B. Eerdmans Publishing Company, 1978, *Contra Arianos*, i.7.
5. *Ideas and Opinions*, p. 324.
6. A. Einstein, *Out of My Later Years*, New York: Philosophical Library, 1950, p. 63.
7. *Ideas and Opinions*, p. 25.

CHAPTER 2

SCIENTIFIC FAITH

THE similarity can be recognised positively in the sense that both science and theology rest ultimately on faith. According to Einstein, "The belief in an external world independent of the perceiving subject is the basis of all natural science."[1] Moreover, "To this there also belongs the faith in the possibility that the regulations valid for the world of existence are rational, that is, comprehensible to reason."[2] Although there is some doubt about the way and the time that the debt was incurred, very few modern scholars would deny that modern science borrowed from Christian theology the basic belief in an external rational world independent of the observer.

The first book of the Bible, Genesis, opens with an anti-mythological statement. "In the beginning, God created the heavens and the earth."[3] This declaration together with the introductory words of John's Gospel make it perfectly clear that God's creating is second to his begetting.[4] "In the beginning was the Word, and the Word was with God, and the Word was God; all things were made by him, and without him was not anything made."[5] It follows, therefore, that the foundations of Christian theology were prepared by God for mankind in his Word before the creation of the World.[6] God made all things by his eternal Word.

God gave substantive existence to the creation. But he did not expose it to the risk of running its own chaotic course only to drop back out of existence.[7] Creation is made not merely to move, but to move in the right direction.[8] By the ordering action of the Word, the creation is sustained. The uncreated Source of rationality, the Word, enables the world to abide securely as a composite

8

created unity. Obeying the Word, things on earth have life and things in the heavens have their order.[9] Consequently, to speak of God, the Father, the Son and the Holy Spirit, as the Object of Christian theology is to recognise, among other things, that the Creator of the universe gave to the creation a distinctive, ordered and harmonious existence which continues through its unique dependence on the triune God. This means that the universe is not self-existent or self-explanatory, but is dependent on the creative action of the triune God.

If a blind eye is turned on this dependence, the dynamically structured reality of the universe may be seen in the light of the basic belief of modern science. Indeed, Einstein could not conceive of a genuine scientist without that profound faith.[10] For him, scientists remain "genuine" in so far as they are not overpowered by their scientific theories. Many theories have a wide range of achievement and an extensive logical manifold. They require forms of reflection that demand considerable understanding and devotion. Hence, it is all too easy to abandon or to ignore their limitations. The temptation is to lose sight of what Einstein called profound scientific faith. To follow or to apply scientific theories is not necessarily to identify with that faith which is the basis of all genuine scientific endeavours.

Clearly, the hydra of apostasy can rear its heads in science as well as theology. Enslavement is a constant danger in scientific research. Sooner or later, all masters grow dependent on their slaves. In particular, scientific theories can enslave and supplant their creators by appeasing them with a comfortable measure of competence. Throughout its history, science has certainly been plagued by the stultifying tendency of current apprehensions of the world to become dominant criteria in the investigation of the natural order. The Ptolemaic system, Euclidean geometry, Newtonian mechanics and the indivisibility of the atom are notable examples. Even Einstein had to contend fiercely with such an adulterant. It took the form of an unjustifiable adherence to Hermann Minkowski's formulation of the special theory of relativity.[11] It is small wonder that Einstein often referred in his discussions to the potency of this particular kind of apostasy.[12]

Scientific faith relates directly to the external world. Of necessity, it remains partially non-formal, although it is neither aformal nor anti-formal. Well-seasoned scientific researchers recognise that it cannot depend exclusively on, or be fashioned solely by, prevalent scientific theories. For instance, Johannes Kepler held a non-formal faith associated with but not restricted by the Copernican system. His profound faith in the existence of natural law gave him the strength to devote decades of hard and patient attention to the investigation of planetary motion. In particular, he had to believe in closed planetary orbits before he could determine their precise shape. In his work Kepler subordinated aspects of public scientific wisdom to his private undefinable notions in order to obtain his three famous laws.

Other examples are not hard to find. Initially, Einstein exercised a blatantly non-formal faith in an extension of the principle of relativity. On this basis, he searched for many years for a theory more general than the special theory of relativity.[13] Originally unspecifiable, his personal commitment to an extension of this principle only found definite expression through his interpretation of the observed equivalence of inertial and gravitational masses.

At the turn of the century, Max Planck resolved what was later to be called the Ultra-violet Catastrophe. He placed his faith in the eventual apprehension of his mere device for new calculations. This artefact insinuated the idea of discrete energy levels of charged harmonic oscillators. It laid the foundation of modern quantum theory. Yet, Planck referred to his innovation as "an act of desperation, for by nature I am peaceful and against dubious adventures."[14]

Only eleven years later, Ernest Rutherford concluded on the strength of his students' astonishing experimental evidence that the atom's central tiny heavy nucleus is surrounded by electrons traversing the vast emptiness of atomic space.¹⁵ Non-formal private faith in a vague model, in the relevance of current theories of statistics and in the importance of almost incredible experimental evidence compelled him to master the mathematics necessary to formulate his preliminary notion of the structure of the atom as resembling that of the solar system.

In general terms, every scientific effort is bound up with an act of pre-reflective faith in the rationality of the universe. The private manifestations of scientific faith are partially non-formal precisely because they deal with cosmic processes. They are non-arbitrary, empirically grounded and heuristically virile. They must never be controlled by the ever changing ideas of historical studies, philosophical investigations or current scientific trends. Certainly, they may be beneficially influenced by those factors, but they should not be restricted by them.

Basically, faith motivates scientific research. The subject and its impact are inseparable. How scientific research is accomplished is inextricably bound up with the reason why it is undertaken. A history of science reconstructed apart from scientific faith cannot represent the foundations of that faith. A philosophy of science posited without reference to perficient faith cannot account for its dynamics. A programme of scientific research hidebound by prevalent scientific theories cannot serve the fundamental purpose of scientific faith. Methods, theories and results developed in science are always determined "where the future is being brewed".¹⁶ They are drastically misunderstood if they are prized as entities of historical and philosophical interest instead of as testimonies to scientific faith. Einstein pointed out that the successes of science give considerable encouragement to this faith.¹⁷

Contrary to popular opinion, private belief can never be entirely eliminated from scientific endeavour. As already indicated, scientific theories are discovered or investigated by individual scientists who hold strong convictions. In this respect, the scientific enterprise resembles the theological reach for the unsearchable riches of Jesus Christ. In both pursuits private faith is subordinate to the objective content of that faith. Indeed, the fact that scientists believe in the eventual transformation of their non-formal notions into definite scientific theories is largely taken for granted by the scientific community. It concentrates on the theories themselves. Likewise, the Church strives for a contemporary doctrinal exposition of God as the Object of Christian theology. What genuine scientists believe, the actual content of their faith, is vitally important to the wider community. Until private belief becomes public wisdom, it remains ineffectual. Einstein's apposite words have strong theological connections, "only a life lived for others is a life worthwhile",[18] although he was speaking from scientific experience.

The scientific community receives from individual scientists necessarily incomplete intimations of the rationality of the universe. They are, so to speak, interpretations of certain events or processes within the natural order. Scientific theories disclose increased surveys of objective reality by which personal scientific faith breathes. But those theories remain silent about the workings of private faith. This thought lay behind Einstein's comment that "the true value of a human being is determined by the measure and sense in which he has attained liberation from self".[19] Once more, Einstein's remark is readily applicable to theologians who, for the most part, study the objective riches of Christian living. Dealing with questions regarding what may be believed, they work for their Lord. By doing so they also discover their own personhood and they learn how to serve their fellow men.

Objectively related to the universe, all scientific theories carry scientists out of the confinement of styles of subjectivism and into the richness and freedom of personal scientific enterprise. To stand on the shoulders of Einstein again, "whoever has undergone the intense experience of successful advance in this domain (science) is moved by profound reverence for the rationality made manifest in existence. By way of the undertaking he achieves a far-reaching emancipation from the shackles of (private) hopes and desires and thereby attains the humble attitude of mind toward the grandeur of reason incarnate in existence, and which, in its profoundest depths, is inaccessible to man".[20] The apprehension bestowed by science is personal though not subjective. It is quite generally supposed to be wholly impersonal. For scientists, every theory has a conceptual frame of reference, a cluster of fundamental concepts and principles in terms of which that realm of nature is described. Although these fundamental terms are not unchangeable and not eternally necessary, their adoption at any particular time seems to be inevitable in the light of their truth-contents. While psychological factors are never completely eliminated from scientific theories, those theories point the scientist beyond his own limitations to greater personal participation in the processes of nature. Modern science claims the obedience of the will, not just the mind's assent.

More mundanely expressed, scientific researchers are not primarily interested in themselves or in the mechanisms or origins of their private faith. Planck's innovation is an excellent example (*vide supra*). The vast majority of scientists are far too busy trying to break new ground to stand back to ponder the intricacies of how they gained novel insights. They are as fully concerned with the rationality of the universe in which they believe as theologians are with the uncreated Source of that rationality who is the Saviour of the world. Invariably, scientists must meet the natural order on its own terms, if they are to attain a greater apprehension of it. The theological correlate is that, in Jesus Christ, God is known as he comes to mankind. Without this Word, theologians are left in the confusion of endless permutations of meaningless words. The proud are scattered in the imagination of their hearts. Similarly, scientists cannot achieve anything by themselves. Without references to experience, they are cut adrift on the high seas of limitless speculation, unable to take bearings. Observation, experimentation and theorising, all of which thrive on experience, will strengthen, however, their already irrepressible commitment to make a greater contact with reality. As Einstein declared, "all knowledge of reality begins and ends in experience".[21]

The natural order, of which scientists are part, discloses its own givenness. This givenness is apprehensible and apprehended only in so far as it is respected and obeyed. It is reflected effectively, but always incompletely, in the language of scientific concepts and theories. Even as individual scientists, the wider community receives those coherent open statements and theories as witnesses to the unity of the objective natural order. In other words, they are assimilated as facets of the concrete meaning of what it is for them to believe in the rationality of the universe.

According to Christian teaching, man does not have the capacity to hear for himself the voice of God. Only the givenness of Jesus Christ could unveil the hiddenness of God. Consequently, as God's unowed offering, the Word became flesh and lived among men.[22] The free gift of Jesus Christ to all mankind is solely attested by the sacred and inspired Scriptures, of which the doctrines of the Churches are guides and interpretations.[23] This unique unmerited givenness is only understandable and understood inasmuch as he is loved and followed.[24] He is foreshadowed in the Law[25] and the Prophets.[26] The record of his life and teachings together with the writings of the Apostles complete the instruction and revelation given for all ages.[27]

The mystery of God cannot be explained but, in the Person of Jesus Christ, what is incomprehensible and inaccessible is made available to men.[28] Systematic theology, therefore, attempts to interpret the Scriptures faithfully, but it does so within severe limitations. The language of theological concepts and doctrines is necessarily inadequate. The object signified is of infinitely greater significance than the signs which signify it.[29] Nevertheless, theological activity, like scientific research, continues in the knowledge that it is prone to error by omission and commission. It hopes that succeeding generations may think more faithfully, incisively and expansively. Most theologians find the confidence in the Word to exercise, as best they can, the God-given freedom to hear and to listen to that Word, and to serve the world for which he died. For them, that is the concrete meaning of what it is to believe in Jesus Christ as Saviour and Lord. They are drawn onward in the knowledge, love and grace of Christ, provided they are obedient to the bound freedom they have been given in and through him.

The givenness of the natural order allows scientists the personal freedom to explore reality. The availability of this freedom is not a consequence of any scientific effort. Its very possibility exists by virtue of what Einstein called "the pre-established harmony between thought and reality",[30] that mysterious harmony of nature into which mankind is born.[31] Where scientists strive independently of nature, they speculate to the detriment of science. They run counter to their native disposition towards the universe. When they choose to meet reality, as indeed they often do, the ground rules are laid down for them. As scientists, they may try to follow those rules or, alternatively, they may decide at any stage and as mere speculators to ignore their existence. Only the former procedure will contribute significantly to scientific apprehension.

The fact that reality is so constituted leaves scientists astonished. For example, the explanation of aspects of nature in terms of quantum theory or the theories of relativity is very partial though often taken by non-scientists as complete. Significantly, great scientific mysteries remain unsolved, mysteries like why do Maxwell's equations, general relativity and Dirac's matrices work, considering that they appear to be intelligent restatements of more fundamental problems? Again, cosmology deals with the mechanisms by which the universe has reached its present state. It provides no answer to the questions of the origin of the matter of the universe. Obviously, modern science is not deprived of indissoluble mystery. In particular, scientists shall never fathom the depths of the mystery of this pre-established harmony. The incomprehensible thing about the universe is its apprehensibility.[32] The inexplicable wonder is that the unfathomable universe is knowable. As "a small piece of nature",[33] the scientific researcher realises that he is in the midst of a continuously self-disclosing world. Reminiscent of the miracle of new life in Christ, this world grants to him the freedom to apprehend it and to live more abundantly in it. The universe is understood to the extent that he appreciates its orders. The only authentic course open to him is the one which binds him to its rationality while freeing him to acquire a new confidence in reality and himself.

If scientific faith motivates research, it does so by fostering trust in the reliability of the universe. In many respects, the reliability of the universe is to the scientist what the faithfulness of God is to the theologian. For scientists, this means that they may place a considerable emphasis upon the effective repeatability or reproducibility of observations and experiments. Of course, logically speaking there is no such thing as rigorous repeatability,[34] but scientists are not restricted to logic. They relate rationally as they theorise and experiment. Rather than trust themselves, they trust the universe. By doing so they closely parallel theologians. Whereas the latter trust in the promise and guidance of the Word of God, the former exercise their freedom to rely heavily on the findings of scientific research, that is, the received intimations of reality. Those findings actually include both empirical and theoretical discoveries.[35]

To return to personal confidence, scientific faith in the natural order delivers scientists from fears, but not the occurrences, of fantasy and delusion.[36] Since their rationality is always insignificant compared to the rationality of the universe, scientists are incapable of strict obedience to the latter rationality. Even scientists cannot keep their promises. In this, they are near neighbours to theologians, who often wander from one distortion to another. Scientists are perpetually open, therefore, to the risk of new fantasies and novel delusions. This is partly why science may be properly referred to as an adventure in faith. Clearly, failure and disillusionment are recurrent hazards on the scientific trail, although the layman is seldom told of the long years of failure that lead to an important discovery. By trusting reality, however, they can still surmount such obstacles to gain greater vistas of its pervasive harmonious order.

At every new turn, the guidance of reality promises to reveal fresh frontiers. There is one God for theologians, and one world for scientists. The scientists' belief that they are not left stranded by their own devices is handsomely rewarded as they depend on the impact of the unfolding universe. Thus, in spite of countless failures, apparent contradictions and persistent paradoxes, they can continue to believe in an objective, ordered and harmonious world.

In fact, modern science's history attests the mystery that scientific faith flourishes in adversity. The struggles of Kepler, Rutherford and Einstein are outstanding examples. Scientific researchers pursue their special interests no matter the extent or severity of private hardship and regardless of the intensity or complexity of public controversies. Coping with errors and disappointments is certainly frustrating, but it is just part of the exciting parcel of modern scientific research.

The immensity, coherence and grandeur of reality are enough to inspire wonder and to keep most scientists wary of the limitations of their theories and experiments. If scientific theories and experiments do anything, they cast some light on the mysterious depths of the universe. They testify to the shining of some light out of those depths, sufficient light to draw scientists to continue searching, to lead them in the way of discovering. Scientific faith does not thrive as prejudiced adherence to theoretical constructions but rather as a ceaseless striving after renewal, a continuous search. The scientific theory is not a terminus. It is a resting place along the way that scientists have to follow.

Probably the greatest obstacles to progress are the reluctance to shed outmoded ways of thinking and acting and the tendency to forget the restrictions of topical types of theorising and experimentation. The former is a product of illegitimate conservatism. The latter is a consequence of immoderate enthusiasm. It is hardly surprising to find that there are equally powerful theological excesses. After all, scientists and theologians are only human beings. Yet, faith is the required antidote because it is prior to all theorising, experimentation, reflection and systematisation.

Like its Christian counterpart, scientific faith is never tentative, although it may fluctuate with the scientific climate. In both cases, the anchor of authentic faith is firmly embedded under the ebb and flow of private manifestations. Apparently resembling more the Noahic Covenant than the New Covenant in Jesus Christ, scientific faith is held fast and exclusively in the rationality of the universe. Scientists are entrusted with this covenant for conveyance to humankind. Scientific faith is bound firmly to the natural order granting to scientific researchers the freedom to experience their personal buoyancy within secured moorings and giving them the openness to respect that there are theological crafts afloat.

NOTES

1. *Ideas and Opinions*, p. 266.
2. *Later Years*, p. 26.
3. *Genesis*, 1.1.
4. *C. Arianos*, ii.2.
5. *John*, 1.1.
6. Athanasius, *de Synodis*, 3.
7. Athanasius, *Contra Gentes*, 41.3.
8. *Ibid.*, 4.5.
9. *Ibid.*, 42.2.
10. *Later Years*, p. 26.
11. *Philosopher-Scientist*, p. 67.
12. *Ideas and Opinions*, pp. 22f.
13. *Philosopher-Scientist*, pp. 65f.
14. M. Planck, quoted in G. Holton, *Thematic Origins of Scientific Thought: Kepler to Einstein*, Cambridge and London: Harvard University Press, 1973, p. 215.
15. Barbara L. Cline, *The Questioners: physicists and the quantum theory*, New York: Thomas Y. Crowell, 1965, pp. 8–13.
16. A. Einstein, quoted in R. W. Clark, *Einstein: The Life and Times*, New York and Cleveland: The World Publishing Company, 1971, p. 131.
17. *Later Years*, p. 64.

18. A. Einstein, quoted by V. G. Hinshaw Jr., in *Philosopher-Scientist*, p. 650.
19. *Ideas and Opinions*, p. 12.
20. *Ibid.*, p. 49.
21. *Ibid.*, p. 271.
22. *John*, 1.14.
23. *C. Gentes*, 1.3.
24. *Ephesians*, 3.18.
25. Athanasius, *de Incarnatione Verbi Dei*, 40.2.
26. *Ibid.*, 12.5.
27. *De Syn.*, 6.
28. *De Incarn.*, 1.2.
29. *C. Gentes*, 21.2.
30. *Ideas and Opinions*, p. 226.
31. *Ibid.*, p. 265.
32. *Later Years*, p. 61.
33. A. Einstein, quoted in *Thematic Origins*, p. 366.
34. G. Thomson, *The Inspiration of Science*, New York: Anchor Books, 1968, p. 11.
35. A. Einstein, in *Einstein: A Centenary Volume*, edited by A. P. French, Cambridge: Harvard University Press, 1979, p. 310.
36. G. Holton, in *A Centenary Volume*, p. 159. See also *Later Years*, p. 61.

CHAPTER 3

SCIENTIFIC KNOWLEDGE

A SIMILARITY between modern science and theological activity can also be found in the natures of scientific and theological knowledge. The aim of science is to describe to the greatest extent possible the rational world independent of the observer.[1] Consequently, scientists try to paint a simplified and intelligible picture of that world.[2] Yet, their conceptual systems are neither arbitrary chaotic sets of abstractions nor absolutely true immutable descriptions. The discoveries of the Copernican system, non-Euclidean geometries, the special theory of relativity and nuclear fission are suitable reminders of the mortality of even the hardiest breed of scientific theory.

Bluntly, "there are no eternal theories in science".[3] Challenging questions, novel concepts and new theories are "born in the painful struggle with old views".[4] That pain is experienced, of course, by scientific researchers who learn that every theory stands and falls as it directs investigation beyond itself toward greater precision and fuller apprehension.[5] In the most significant cases, the new theory shows the merits as well as the limitations of the old theory. It also allows scientists to regain old concepts from a broader but restricted logical basis.[6] If scientific knowledge were a mere inventory of facts, it might still be useful, but it would not be pursued with passion. Few persons can summon any real enthusiasm for reading time-tables, telephone directories and the like. Clearly, for science to nurture devotion in its researchers, its changing theories must answer a fundamental need. Their development, being largely conditioned by considerations springing from scientific ground, gratifies the desire to apprehend, the will to search, and the need to know. Nevertheless, to apprehend something is to see it in its place within a particular framework and to appreciate, as far as possible, the limitations of that location. In general, each scientific generation is characterised by idiosyncrasies and sympathies which colour their choice as to which aspects of a problem they will ignore and what elements they will investigate. Scientific knowledge cannot be poured like milk in a jug from one generation to another. Each scientific generation trains the senses, exercises the intellect and distinctively subordinates both of these to the rationality of the universe. Modern science is much more than mere facts or formulae. It is a way of commitment, enterprise and change.

The aim of systematic theology is also necessarily limited for God is beyond comparison.[7] Systematic theology does not try to solve, nor does it ignore, the reality of the mystery of God.[8] Its object is not to encapsulate meanings with formulae or concepts.[9] The purpose of theological activity is not to provide instant doctrinal relief for all the ailments of Christian thinking. Its intention is less ambitious but more courageous. Like that of scientific theories, its validity resides in its capacity to point beyond itself to a fuller apprehension of the inexhaustible reality of God. Yet, God the Creator is invisible and inaccessible to originated things.[10] As Athanasius confessed so long ago, "... all created beings and especially we who are men, find it impossible to speak adequately concerning the things that are ineffable".[11]

The heart of the matter is the mystery that divine activity cannot be measured by the nature of men.[12] God cannot be known by the unaided powers of human knowledge. He is known by his own decisions and actions. Human interpretations, therefore, always fall short of the biblical notion of God which, by means of things known to men, allows them to apprehend a little of what they can never comprehend.[13,14] Hence, the humble task of systematic theology is to enable Christian thinking to shed more readily the encumbrances of answers that are too small for him who is the Truth.[15] Its work is to find where the theological shoe pinches and to make room for the reflective movements of Christian living.

All scientific theories have truth-contents commensurate with their realms of validity. Every scientific concept or theory relates to the rationality of the universe. Indeed, that rationality is the only truth to which it can relate. Whereas for theology the Word is the eternal Truth, for modern science the rationality of the universe is the singular truth. In no sense is it provisional. The laws of nature are already invariant as scientists search for a deeper understanding of them. This truth reveals itself in scientific concepts and theories as meaning, that is, as truth-content to be assimilated. To borrow Einstein's words, "a system has a truth-content according to the certainty and completeness of its coordination-possibility to the totality of experience".[16] The concrete meaning or the truth-content of a theory is the way in which that theory succeeds in ordering and correlating definite ranges of sense experiences.[17]

Modern science points to the rationality of the universe with its own restricted theoretical systems. Those systems express themselves most effectively, but always incompletely and openly, in mathematical terms. Scientific theories are not, however, speculative in origin.[18] They are logically free creations of the scientific mind, but they are based on sense experiences.[19] As Einstein pointed out, the grasping of scientific truth is not possible without empirical basis.[20] It is widely recognised that the deeper science penetrates reality and the more extensive and embracing its theories become the less empirical knowledge is needed to determine those theories. Nevertheless, all scientific theories are ultimately empirically grounded. This grounding endows them with real content. They survey real knowledge but with limited logic and precision.

Perhaps surprising to many scientists, disciplined theologians rarely depart in their theologising from the data of Christian experience, that is, the reality of God in their lives.[21] To select a well-known example, the doctrine of the Trinity was not officially accepted in the Church

SCIENTIFIC KNOWLEDGE 23

until the fourth century. It does not appear as such in the New Testament. Yet, this doctrine grew out of the early Church's experience of God as the Father, the Son and the Holy Spirit. Its existence is not due to the illicit private allegations of a group of presumptuous theologians. This doctrine resulted from the freedom of objective reflection on the personal Christian experience of the early Church. The trinitarian formulation and its mysterious "three-in-one" language, like all systematic theology, is an attempt to give ordered expression to experience. In this respect, modern quantum theory with its wave-particle descriptions plays a somewhat similar role in science. The main point is that Christian experience always precedes theological activity which surveys real knowledge incompletely but openly. Theology rests securely on empirical knowledge.

The emergence of the doctrine of the Trinity in the fourth century came from neither a need to define God nor a decisive new revelation, but from the experienced reality of God. This doctrine represented the desire to express what had been the Church's worship and experience of God from its beginning. It was built from the mortar and bitumen of the Incarnation and Pentecost. The reality of Jesus' humanity could not be denied in the light of the experience of the first disciples. Justice could not be done to it by simply describing Jesus as man or God or as part man and part God. As surely as non-formal scientific faith required thinking of the electron as a wave and also as a particle, so partially non-formal Christian faith demanded new ways of thinking of God as the Father and the Son. Indeed, the latter became necessary modes of speaking of God for the first disciples through the compelling reality of Jesus Christ in their lives.

Again, with the experience of Pentecost, the early Church discovered that God was present in their lives in a profoundly powerful and new way. Still, it was not entirely new. It intensified their sense of the presence of the one God whom they had known through Jesus. This discovery of the early Church was more concrete than the scientific revelation that the classical particulate behaviour of the free electron is co-essential with the wave character of the electron. Gifted with this blend of the familiar and the original, the early Church spoke informally of God as the Father, the Son and the Holy Spirit. While it is correct to say, therefore, that the formal doctrine of the Trinity is not present in the New Testament, the worship and experience of the Trinity is faithfully recorded there. This experience made it both necessary and possible to formulate the doctrine of the Trinity when the Church in mission attempted to communicate to the world what it believed about God.

The doctrine of the Trinity, like any other Christian doctrine, is empirically grounded in historic data that are recorded in the sacred and inspired Scriptures. All theology appeals to empirical data, to a set of events which occurred in history. At the centre of theology stands the historical existence of Jesus of Nazareth. Those events occurred in space and time, and they tell of what men saw, smelled, heard, tasted and touched. Christian doctrines survey those events with limited logic and precision, but they can only be known to do this in so far as they are anchored in personal Christian experience. Logical investigation cannot reveal the connection between theological concepts and Christian experience. It can only show how concepts relate to one another. Their anchorage in Christian life endows them with real living content.[22] Both modern science and theology represent human activities that benefit from the full impact of experience. Without experience, science and theology remain speculation. As creative responses to the real world, they free the individual from the fears of fantasy and delusion. Each offers a way of life that involves commitment rooted in action. They have a common desire to remove anthropocentric images that stand between the person and reality. These disciplines encourage creative individuals to act on the hope that personal life based on an empirical knowledge is more real than anything that a closed conceptual system has to offer.

Precisely because scientific theories rest on empirical knowledge, scientific knowledge is created when those theories are either discovered or assimilated. To use an extended analogy, a scientist responds to the presence of the universal rational field by reorienting the concepts of one of the established theories. He initiates this response with a heuristic departure from that theory. This reaction is a creative act of faith, probably involving a non-formal, perhaps non-articulate, concept.[23] The first half of a conceptual hysteresis loop is completed when that notion intimates its ability to re-structure and to enlarge a known range of sense experiences. This act of discovery prompts a formalising return which carries apprehension beyond the old theory to its successor. By their theories and instruments scientists have enlarged the world in which they live until it has become immensely richer than that inhabited by their primitive predecessors.

What has just been described is, in fact, the husk of Christian living. Its kernel is Jesus Christ who is the Way, the Truth and the Life.[24] If, in the preceding description, the Word is heard from his rightful centrality, he is also recognised as the Truth who irradiates all the creation. Christians respond to this living Truth by realigning themselves to point more nearly along the Way to God. Throughout their lives they offer their diverse personal responses to his presence as ventures in faith that cannot always be fully expressed in words. Nevertheless, when faithfully carried to completion, these reactions culminate in a re-ordering and an expansion of their lives. Thus, they fulfil Jesus' promise that he came that men may have life and have it abundantly.[25] Since the acts of Christian faith bring with them enrichment of life through its reorientation, it is hardly surprising to find that an echo of this rationality is captured by modern scientific research.

During scientific research it is difficult, if not impossible, to isolate the venture in faith from the unfolding of knowledge. In any case, a full conceptual loop has to be traversed, so to speak, before a new scientific theory can emerge as the next point of departure. Since, in this view, scientific theories are evidently testimonies to scientific faith, the latter cannot possibly be irrational or antirational. Actually, scientific faith is rational only in so far as it derives from the rationality of the universe. The well-known theological correlate is that the rationality of Christian faith rests exclusively on the Word of God. Moreover, any established theory, like any Christian doctrine, initially involved an act of faith. This act enabled scientists or theologians to apprehend some process or event. At the same time, the act opened up the possibility for scientists or theologians to make those phenomena apprehensible to others. To put it in a nutshell, scientific faith is like Christian faith in that both breed knowledge, that is, scientific researchers and theologians believe in order to understand.

Both scientific faith and theological faith are concerned, therefore, with the re-orientation of conceptual systems, the expansion of apprehension. The one has to do with the object of faith, the universe of which scientific theories speak, the other with the one God who is the Source of all reality. As already noted, however, it is of the natures of God and of his universe that they are apprehensible and apprehended solely by self-disclosures. Whereas God has made himself known to man in the Word incarnate, the universe declares itself to scientists in its own distinctive way. Neither scientific researchers nor theologians can think anything out for themselves without external stimulation. There is no logic of scientific or theological discovery. An infinite number of tests are required to establish the logical necessity of a scientific or theological concept. There are no watertight theories or systems, but there is enough empirical knowledge to warrant a decision of faith. No general scientific or theological procedure can be set down for scientists or theologians to follow. Modern science or theology does not obey a simple law of continuous progress.[26]

A full comparative study of the cited achievements of Kepler, Planck, Rutherford and Einstein will readily support the scientific content of those statements. It will also illustrate how a non-logical leap, a chance discovery, an unexpected result or an intuitive hunch can transport a scientist through an existing conceptual barrier. The effectiveness of such diverse breakthroughs in scientific research indicates that knowledge of reality, like knowledge of God, is not merely an option to be taken up as it suits the individual. Scientific knowledge occurs where there is actual experience that reality discloses its undiscovered order. Reminiscent of Christian teaching, scientific knowledge presents itself to the receptive hidden qualities of the open mind in such a manner that the scientist cannot fail to grasp its significance, but personal freedom is never abused.

The scientific attitude, the manner in which scientists go about their work, is just as important to science as scientific results. The individual scientist must have the single-mindedness to respond to the intimations of reality and the personal freedom to serve that matches the rigours of relentless industry. For example, some histories of science report that Galileo's opponents refused to view Jupiter's moons as if they were perversely obstinate. In fact, they sensed, even if they disagreed with, Galileo's profoundly different response to the universe. His research represented something more important than a contribution to the theory of planetary motion. Galileo advocated a new attitude to life and knowledge. Basically, he proposed that the scientist look and listen very carefully to the natural order.

Probably surprising to many laymen, modern science demands an unqualified obedience to the determinate universe. This obedience does not violate the person of the scientist. On the contrary, his great freedom to function as a child of the universe is a privilege through which he can find self-fulfilment. Scientific research is much more satisfying than mere neutral inquiry. Inevitably, scientists bring certain presuppositions to their investigations, but the major strength or excitement of science is its ability to transcend educated expectation. The compelling character of the rationality of the universe shatters their limited expectations by disclosing the intriguing possibility of reformulating current theory.

While it is certainly true that nature favours the prepared mind, knowledge does not take place under conditions that are completely controlled by the scientist. Scientific theories are mined not minted. There are always unknown factors operative during any scientific investigation. Knowledge occurs under those circumstances where the scientist is confronted by reality. In other words, science chooses the scientist, that is, destiny places the scientist at a turning point in the development of the human intellect.[27] The close parallel to Christian living can hardly be missed. Experience that God speaks is the locus of knowledge of God. It takes place only when and where divine revelation occurs. God calls the person to serve as he wills, and the Word of God, the uncreated Source of rationality, teaches the person how to live at the melting point of the salvation of mankind.

Einstein expressed his unshakable belief in the knowability of the universe in terms of the intuitive relation. "The relational structure of an independent reality can be cognized by virtue of the pre-established harmony between thought and reality".[28] This pervasive harmony imposes the important restriction that, for a scientific theory to be complete, every element of the correlated realm of reality must have a counterpart in that theory. The attainment of scientific truth, therefore, would require the comprehension of all reality whose processes and events are so enmeshed in the universal manifold as to provide a dynamically ordered and harmonious unity. But scientists are always immersed in more sense experiences than they can cope with at any given moment. Hence, they must repeatedly decide to disregard some of them and to attend exclusively to others. From the totality of their sense impressions scientists attend to those only which can be ordered, measured or formulated. Their methods of simplification allow them to deal with severely restricted realms of the real world. In this view, modern science is only capable of following in the footsteps of the truth.

SCIENTIFIC KNOWLEDGE

For theologians the Truth is inseparable from the Incarnation. The Word became flesh.[29] His task is to bear witness to the truth. For this was he born; for this he came into the world.[30] Christianity is, therefore, a revealed religion, not a human invention. Convictions respecting it are inscrutably based on partially non-formal faith, for the Word has no parallel with others.[31] Those convictions, however, become more and more articulate as they are practised and learned in the laboratory of daily life and work. The Word became incarnate as the Truth to be learned and lived.

This requires reflection. To borrow Einstein's description of scientific theories, theology "is the attempt at the posterior reconstruction of existence by the process of conceptualization".[32] It cannot be otherwise since, in their apprehensions of the Son of God and in and through his life, theologians must follow the Word incarnate. While the acreage of systematic theology is as large as Christian experience itself, it can only aspire to co-extension with the Truth. Jesus Christ declares in his Person that God's truth is of universal scope and objectivity.[33] Whether or not Jesus is personally known, understood or believed, he remains the Truth.[34] Consequently, his rationality subordinates all ventures in faith and reason[35] and all theological activity humbly glimpses the Truth in a poorly prepared mirror.

The pervasive structure of the universe is infinitely greater than what scientists can define or quantify. Indeed, it presents through the intuitive relation all that scientists seek to apprehend. When they investigate the unknown or encounter the unexpected, they are confronted and guided by its comprehensive reality. The pre-established harmony between thought and reality is effectual through personal intuition. Intuition allows the practising scientist "to differentiate clearly the fundamentally important, that which is really basic",[36] from the plethora of concepts and experiences that tend to congest the mind and divert it from the essential. It enables the scientist to frame proper questions, to make legitimate associations and to construct forms independently before they can find them in things. Intuition cannot be defined. It involves a mediated type of knowledge which informs an appetitive sensibility to non-quantitative tokens of reality.

Clearly, the intuitive relation implies that scientific knowledge is not wholly explicit. Such knowledge is never "objective" in the sense that its content is entirely determined by observation and experiment. Scientific theories refer to the limitless universal implications of their subject. The relation of the intuitive and explicit components of knowledge caters for the existence of those non-formal unspecifiable notions that are so important in scientific research. Theoretical statements and their vague but authentic fore-runners relate to reality in an indefinite variety of ways. They imply more than their originators first extracted from them. Their heuristic connectivities preclude pre-established rules to determine the fate of a theory or hypothesis in the event of experimental failure. In any case, scientific wisdom generally supervenes. For example, throughout his scientific life, Einstein held firmly to the conviction that "a scientific theory is more impressive the greater the simplicity of its premises, the more different kinds of things it relates, and the more extended is its area of applicability".[37]

Scientists often judge a concept or a theory on the basis of non-formal tokens of reality, including simplicity, correlativity and applicability. As far as they are concerned, the validity of a theory depends on more than its local legitimation. It relies also on its broader capacity to reveal reality or to guide an intuited sense of hidden implications. Many theologians depend on very similar characteristics in their investigations and expositions of the doctrines of the churches. Basically, the mysterious harmony into which the scientist is born enables him through intuition to feed a growing apprehension of the natural order and to make ever greater contact with independent reality.[38]

As discussed earlier, God and the universe are knowable through themselves. When the theologian or scientist experiences this, he is emancipated, liberated to apprehend

God or the universe, respectively. Knowledge of reality has truth-content precisely because it is determined in theology by God and in science by the universe. It cannot be the truth since it is knowledge confined by the frailties of scientific or theological reasoning. In science, awesome universal references are always carried in awkward human relevancies, while theology refers to the uncreated Creator using the creations of creatures.

Scientific concepts and theories are not even adequate to grasp the knowability of this comprehensive rationality. Much the same can be said of Christian doctrines. Yet, wider cognitive powers than traditional conceptions of knowledge seem to be at work in both scientific research and theological activity. Consequently, where knowledge breaks through into science or theology, there is no cause for an immoderate sense of personal achievement. As Einstein modestly echoed the fellowship of the universal Church, "the work of the individual scientist is so bound up with that of his scientific predecessors and contemporaries that it appears almost as an impersonal product of his generation".[39] In addition to this corporate dimension, there is also, of course, the commitment of the scientist or theologian to the rationality of the universe or its Source, respectively. This commitment carries the person, no matter the immensity of his own achievement, to the limitations of his scientific theories or theological contributions, as the case may be. Such an experience is at once humbling and challenging.

To repeat, scientific faith and Christian faith have to do with the reorientation of rationality, the expansion of apprehension. Whereas Christians are free to enjoy the abundance of life, scientists are able to explore without compromise the truth of the universe. This truth is a creative truth, and knowledge of it is creative. Scientific faith breeds scientific knowledge. It is, therefore, a completely rational activity. But the truth of the universe is also an empirical truth, and knowledge of it is factual. Scientific faith is co-essentially empirical. It follows that this kind of faith has both an empirical and a rational truth-content. In fact, the two must not be separated.[40] What is actually involved is a creative truth-content. The empirical and rational constituents of scientific knowledge are, as it were, two sides of the same coin. And once again, by making the appropriate changes, the theologian can provide a rather detailed parallel description of Christian theology as living knowledge through its empirical grounding and rational basis in Jesus Christ, the Word incarnate.

It is probably more instructive to speak of scientific wisdom than of scientific knowledge, although scientists tend to object to such terminology because of its religious associations. With decades of "anxious searching in the dark"[41] behind him, Einstein was persuaded that "knowledge exists in two forms — lifeless, stored in books, and alive in the consciousness of men. The second form of existence is after all the essential one; the first, indispensable as it may be, occupies only an inferior position".[42] Most scientists are suitably sensitised to the fact that modern science depends on working knowledge. Experimental and observational researches are obviously practical pursuits, but so is theoretical science. Einstein's general theory of relativity is a superb example. Scientific wisdom not only conveys knowledge but it also possesses potentialities for action, like the detection of the bending of starlight or radio waves by the sun. The composite of the empirical and rational elements of knowledge, known as scientific wisdom, is alive within the consciousness of the scientist equipping him for his scientific expeditions. It is the craft by which he travels across both the rich pastures and the arid deserts of scientific exploration. To journey in this way is the very meaning of scientific knowledge with its accent clearly on action. Christian knowledge means following in the truth of Jesus Christ, and scientific knowledge involves pursuing the truth of the rationality of the universe. The former represents the theologian's living trust in the uncreated Source of all rationality while the latter is the scientist's concrete trust in the natural order. Authentic tenable trust is necessarily founded on the respective truth. As science's history shows, there is no concept, theory or datum, no genuinely scientific knowledge which does not have the sign of this truth, that is, some indication of the order and harmony of nature. Because scientists follow this truth, search in the light of a knowledge of reality, and therefore expand their rationalities, they enlarge their confidence in the meaning of the order and harmony of all natural events and processes. Like theologians, they become surer of the meaning of the ground of all existence as they live in the midst of their surveys and co-ordinations. As new uncharted continents appear before them, scientists sense that wonder which comes from experiencing what it is to know even in part the truth of the universe. It is, as already noted, a liberation from self. Through intuition the scientist is led into truth, freed "to find a peace and security which he cannot find in the narrow whirlpool of (merely) personal experience".[43]

By trusting and knowing something of the rationality of the universe the scientist enacts the meaning of scientific research. He is too busy to ask what that meaning is. The believing scientist resembles the theologian in that both act out the meaning of their lives. When scientific believers assert that the rationality of the universe is the scientific way, they are not presenting science as one possible response to the natural order. For them it is *the* way, just as for theologians Jesus is *the* way. The scientist or the theologian affirms that his way is grounded in the acknowledgement of reality, its independence and its rationality. Each claims ontological backing for such an approach to the world. In both cases, the way is valid for all or it is valid for no one. The scientist knows that the work he does gives him a legitimate place and activity within the natural order of which he is a little part. Where scientific faith reigns, there is also instated through trust in the universe a peace and a security that come before apprehension, and that, for this reason, make the scientific enterprise possible. With this peace and security, scientific researchers are well equipped to pursue the scientific way, truth and life. They can also begin to appreciate that by doing so their activities remarkably resemble those of theologians who follow Jesus Christ.

NOTES

1. *Ideas and Opinions*, p. 282.
2. *Ibid.*, pp. 225f.
3. A. Einstein and L. Infeld, *The Evolution of Physics*, New York: Simon and Schuster, 1938, p. 75.
4. *Ibid.*, p. 26.
5. *Ideas and Opinions*, p. 284.
6. *Evolution of Physics*, pp. 151f.
7. *C. Arianos*, i.57.
8. *Ibid.*, i.41.
9. *Ibid.*, ii.3.
10. *Ibid.*, i.63.
11. Athanasius, *Ad Serapionem*, 1.17, translation by C. R. B. Shapland, *The Letters of Saint Athanasius concerning The Holy Spirit*, London, The Epworth Press, 1951, p. 106.
12. *C. Arianos*, i.26.
13. *Ibid.*, i.23.
14. *Ad Serap.*, 2.6.
15. *C. Arianos*, ii.1.
16. *Philosopher-Scientist*, p. 13.
17. *Later Years*, pp. 62f.
18. *Ideas and Opinions*, p. 246.
19. *Later Years*, p. 60.
20. A. Einstein, in *Albert Einstein: The Human Side*, edited by Helen Dukas and B. Hoffman, Princeton: Princeton University Press, 1979, p. 29.
21. *De Incarn.*, 57.1-3.
22. *John*, 7.17.
23. *Philosopher-Scientist*, p. 7.
24. *John*, 14.6.
25. *Ibid.*, 10.10.
26. H. Bondi, in *Problems of Scientific Revolutions*, edited by R. Harré, Oxford: Clarendon Press, 1975, p. 1.
27. *Ideas and Opinions*, p. 254.
28. V. F. Lenzen, in *Philosopher-Scientist*, p. 363. See also *Ideas and Opinions*, p. 226.
29. *John*, 1.14.
30. *John*, 17.37.
31. *C. Arianos*, ii.6.
32. *Ideas and Opinions*, p. 44.
33. *C. Arianos*, ii.5.
34. *Ibid.*, ii.9.

35. *Ibid.*, ii.2.
36. Ilse Rosenthal-Schneider, in *Philosopher-Scientist*, pp. 144f.
37. *Ibid.*, p. 33.
38. *Ideas and Opinions*, p. 265.
39. A. Einstein, quoted in *Life and Times*, p. 95.
40. *Einstein: A Centenary Volume*, p. 310.
41. *Ideas and Opinions*, pp. 288f.
42. *Ibid.*, p. 80.
43. *Ibid.*, pp. 225f.

CHAPTER 4

SCIENTIFIC COMMUNICATION

THE similarity between science and theology is reflected in their modes of communication. Both Christian theology and scientific research begin and end with a desire to apprehend,[1] a need to believe[2] and a will to search.[3] "Throughout all our efforts", wrote Einstein and Infeld, "in every dramatic struggle between old and new views, we recognise the eternal longing for understanding, the ever firm belief in the harmony of our world, continually strengthened by the increasing obstacles to comprehension".[4] These remarks refer to the personal activities of scientists, but theologians are also engaged in an essentially personal process. Whereas scientists are part of the eternal mystery between reality and thought, theologians are immersed in the ineffable mystery between God and man. Each process or "delicate little plant, aside from stimulation, stands mainly in need of freedom; without this it goes to wreck and ruin without fail. It is a very grave mistake to think that the enjoyment of seeing and searching can be promoted by means of coercion and a sense of duty".[5] To breathe, Christian theology and scientific research must have the invigorating atmosphere of freedom.

Athanasius provided an excellent image of Christian freedom which, with few changes, captures the essence of scientific freedom.[6] The world is like the sea to Christians (or scientists). Persons float on this sea, as with the wind, through their own free-will, for everyone directs his course according to his will. Either under the pilotage of the Word (or the universe), he enters into peace, or, laid hold on by subjective currents he suffers shipwreck, and is in peril by storm. For as in the ocean there are currents and storms, so in the world there are speculations and conflicts. But having their senses exercised in self-control and being strong in Christian (or scientific) faith, the committed continue and are delivered by awakening to the Lord (or the rationality of the universe).

To elaborate on Einstein's thoughts, scientific research is based on the freedom of the universe to disclose itself to the scientist and on the "inner freedom" of the scientist to respond to these disclosures. The latter freedom is a gift. It is not earned but it is part of the givenness of the universe. The theologian claims that this freedom is an aspect of the creation which God in his freedom wills for man. Above all, this means that, where scientific faith or Christian faith is operative, concrete events are taking place, history is being made. Substantive reactions occur where the freedom of the universe and the personal freedom of the scientist intersect, and when the freedom of God and the personal freedom of the Christian meet.

Whenever science has opted for power instead of freedom, it has been usurping the rationality of the universe. Exclusive claims of certainty and finality for its theories have led scientists on false trails. Only by way of self-giving service can they obey this rationality. Yet, the scientific community for all its fantasies and failures, has never wholly obscured this unique rationality. But no-one was ever argued into the scientific community. It takes more than intellectual assent to become a scientist. To learn how to research scientifically, the person must follow this inclusive rationality. The mind and the will go mysteriously hand in hand in this personal adventure.

Scientific faith is, as it were, the universe's mystery breaking through at those intersections, while Christian faith is the experience of God's mystery revealing itself in the work and Person of Jesus Christ. Without those breakthroughs the inexhaustible mysteries of the universe would remain forever inaccessible and invisible, and modern science could never have arisen. For scientific research rests on faith in the rationality of the universe. When scientists speak of the harmony and order of the natural world, they are pointing to the wonder that the world is not a static formless chaos, but that it exists as a dynamically ordered harmonious universe.

Theological thought acknowledges that the ways and thoughts of God are not those of man.[7] But in the birth, death, resurrection and ascension of Jesus Christ, God revealed himself once for all. Theological activity is centred on the Word incarnate from whom rationality radiates to order and to harmonise the whole of the creation. Christian faith is man's privileged reply to the historical existence of the Word of God. As the only acceptable answer from the human side to the New Covenant in Jesus Christ, it is invariably associated with the formation of a fellowship of believers. It is a community of the faithful, a group who do not exist for themselves, but who have a message to proclaim to the world outside of this communion. This fellowship is the Church, the Body of Christ, which has a historical form and content dependent upon its concrete obedience to God's historical work and word in the Person of Jesus Christ.

Scientific research has always a historical dimension in the cosmological sense that the invariant determinate laws of nature structure space-time and govern the scientific enterprise. Everything to which science witnesses depends on those laws. In this view, therefore, scientific research represents the scientist's response within and to the historic continuous processes and events of the universe. Thus, the historical character of modern science makes its presence felt in the investigations and communications of the scientific community. This fraternity reaches across the divides of culture, nation and generation. Indeed, by means of this global brotherhood, modern science serves not its own purposes but the non-scientific world in so far as that community reacts obediently through its researches and publications to the rationality of the universe.

Obedience to the objectivity of the universe is the scientist's reply to the questions that are put to him by nature. For scientific research to be a breed of obedience, the universe must present scientists with a choice, just as the Gospel of Jesus Christ confronts persons with a decision. In both cases, the choice is between trust and unbelief, knowledge and ignorance, wisdom and superstition, peace and fear. Einstein, for example, was convinced that "scientific research can reduce superstition by encouraging people to think in terms of cause and effect".[8] In other words, scientific endeavour relates the scientist to the universe as an integral part of the natural order, that is, in accordance with the invariant determinate laws of nature. Athanasius said as much centuries ago while discussing how man must respond to God in ways appropriate to God.[9]

In scientific research there can be no neutrality beyond the rationality of the universe. Consequently, as the scientist searches and reports, he acknowledges his obligation towards independent reality. In this way he escapes from private life into the public world of responsible objective thought and action. The theologian must also rise above private senses and interpretations through the objective Word of God,[10] who nourishes the sense of Christian fellowship. Without this affinity for corporate identity, scientific research and faith revert, slowly but surely, to mere superstition and contrivance. In contra-distinction, those scientific researchers, who believe in the intelligible universe, follow its rationality, are guided by intuition, contribute to and are enlightened by the public corpus of scientific knowledge.

All scientists are free to trust the rationality of the universe and to apprehend that rationality, as all Christians are at liberty to believe in and to understand the Word of God. Those two freedoms, however, are not sufficient for scientific research or Christian living. By using some or all of the five senses, everyone trusts implicitly the rationality of the universe or its Creator. Moreover, the freedom to believe in God or the intelligible universe is necessarily accompanied by the identification of definite historical events or recurrent manifestations of universal order, that is, by a recognition of empirical knowledge. Obviously, trust without empirical knowledge would be groundless and, therefore, null and void. Yet, much speculation throughout the history of civilisation has rested on both an empirical knowledge and a trust of nature. Clearly, other factors were required in order to induce the birth of modern science.

One of those factors is the freedom of public accountability. This freedom is as important to science as the additional freedom to proclaim the Gospel is to theology. By their self-disclosures the universe and God declare themselves to sentient creatures. However, to remain faithful to the universe or its Creator, as the case may be, scientists or Christians must also announce publicly their new discoveries of universal order. They are committed by action and thought either to the elucidation of the rationality of the universe or to the proclamation of the revelation of God in Jesus Christ. Scientific researchers, therefore, are rarely indifferent to the modes of communication of scientific results.

Where there is scientific faith, the scientific wonders of the world are published for all to ponder and to appreciate. When there is Christian faith, the miracle of Jesus Christ is proclaimed for everyone to know and to share. In spite of the "Horation" deficiency, the inability to account for many important things in heaven and earth, theologians have the inalienable liberty to express their knowledge and trust in the Word of God, and scientists are irrepressibly free to report the details and results of their researches. This public accountability of trust in the rationality of the universe and of apprehension of that rationality is the compelling reason for the whole of the academic scientific literature. It does not take a genius to draw up a long list of the ways in which scientists have allowed internal strife and deep division to divert and to delay the pursuit of truth. In all generations some scientists have distorted the message of science and alienated many people. Nevertheless, it is to the scientific community that the world owes the evidence against its own creations. Modern science is the medium in and through which the rationality of the universe communicates with man. To be a scientist is not merely to receive as valid certain teaching, nor even simply to accept membership in a particular society. It is to relate to the universe in its rationality and to find personal fulfilment from its reality as disclosed within the scientific community. That community is the organ of communication of the rationality of the universe.

This rationality must not be judged, however, by that community's performance. The universe achieves the dynamic order without coercion. It is inconsistent, therefore, to praise its rationality's profound regard for personhood and, in the same breath, to condemn it for not imposing uniformity and perfection on the scientific community. The tendencies to foist arbitrary authority on the theories and results of scientific research and a degrading submissiveness on scientists effectively deny that authority which resides in the universe's readiness to serve, not to dominate. This unique, universal authority is the universe reaching out in service to humankind. The only test of the propriety of its claim to authority is the quality and intensity of the service rendered.

Equivalently, the theological literature represents the Church's most precise form of proclamation. It has developed technical language with its own special history in anticipation of those circumstances that require the rigorous exposition of the deep things of Christian faith. Above all, it is a language of the Bible and of Christian tradition involving concepts by which the Church has received, defended and proclaimed through the ages its apprehension of God and his creation.

Ineluctably, scientific public accountability within the scientific community also needs technical language. All scientific disciplines have their own unique histories to which they bear witness with the continuities of their concepts and theories. This means that the modes of communication are progressively specialised. According to Einstein, "the whole of science is nothing more than a refinement of everyday thinking".[11] Modern science counteracts and overcomes the tendency of systems of thought to become fixed, inflexible and tied up inextricably with the cultures in which they originate or with which they are associated. As far as Einstein was concerned, "Scientific concepts begin with those used in ordinary language for the affairs of everyday life, but they develop quite differently. They are transformed and lose the ambiguity associated with them in ordinary language, gaining in rigour so that they may be applied to scientific thought".[12] The length, vector and tensor illustrate Einstein's remarks.

Basically, scientific concepts and theories are founded on measurements and observations that lend themselves to mathematical formulation.[13] In general, the history of science may be described as the expanding expression of the sum total of its knowledge. Somewhat like the terms of a geometric series, science spans sequentially greater domains within the natural order. In the historical process, it is transformed by the inclusion of higher terms, so to speak. The resulting unifications of scientific theories are responses to the unity of the universe. Science expresses itself most effectually, but always incompletely, in mathematical terms. By doing so it depends, as Einstein implied, on the conceptual continuity of scientific knowledge, that is, on a continuing refinement of the ancient inventions of language, writing and counting.

It is evident, then, that scientists find in the language of their discipline the freedom to be publicly accountable for their scientific faith and wisdom. When they communicate through lectures, text-books or scientific papers, they relate invariably to the unique history of their subjects. Every concept and theory to which they refer has a concrete but complex case history. This complexity arises primarily because scientists organise their conceptual reactions to the natural order in ways similar to the co-ordination of muscular and visual responses during skilful activities.[14] The important point is that non-articulate conceptual elements are responsible for the fluidity of concepts and theories. This comes as no great surprise to theologians. Athanasius, for example, wrote of the non-articulate nature of conceptualisation in the fourth century.[15]

Just as the description of a person cannot acquaint one with him, so a definition of a scientific concept cannot provide an exhaustive understanding of it. Scientific researchers must live alongside it to learn how it behaves in a variety of contexts. The nature of the chemical bond is an excellent example. This means that scientific theories and concepts, like their theological correlates, are never comprehensively exposable to lucid critical inspection. The elusive empirical connectivity of a concept or theory is the heuristic factor in its development. An authentic study of its case history must, therefore, take this factor into account.

The heuristic coefficient of scientific knowledge nourishes the language of a scientific discipline as a living language, a language of public accountability in which scientists are obliged to report. In those languages, modern science has discovered, assimilated and published its knowledge across the centuries and the continents of the world. And, if the discoveries of science and its commitment to objective reality are to continue to be expressed as effectively as possible, then mathematics vitalised by conceptual continuities and empirical connectivities must inevitably and continuously form the bases of scientific languages.

To repeat the obvious, when scientists present their theories as they communicate their faith in the intelligible universe, they speak or write in the special languages of their disciplines. To report otherwise would necessarily be at the expense of clarity and precision. Indeed, the very existence of scientific languages testifies that there are certain concepts and theories that can be best expressed directly in those languages. It is imperative, therefore, that this be done in the academic scientific journals, the learned presence of august societies and the text-books of science. But there is also another side to scientific publication.

Einstein, like many scientists, was convinced that "it is of great importance that the general public be given an opportunity to experience — consciously and intelligently — the efforts and results of scientific research. It is not sufficient that each result be taken up, elaborated and applied by a few specialists in the field. Restricting the body of knowledge to a small group deadens the philosophical spirit of a people and leads to spiritual poverty".[16] Clearly, Einstein was opposed to the idea that scientific faith and wisdom should be restricted to scientific institutions and academic literature. Modern science is uniquely part of the more general pattern of cultural advancement. Scientists are creative persons who think and judge independently. They are wholly committed to increasing mankind's apprehension of the natural order. Without them and their artistic, philosophical and theological cousins, "the upward development of society is as unthinkable as the development of the individual personality without the nourishing soil of the community".[17]

Modern science is meaningless unless it exists for the sake of mankind. Science must address itself, therefore, to the world in which it lives. It does so by presenting scientific wisdom in an authentic but acceptable popular manner. Yet, comparatively few scientists have both the gifts and the opportunities to communicate their awareness of the joys, excitements, anticipations and achievements of modern science. Nevertheless, through the industry and dedication of a small competent minority, popular accounts of the progress of science are made available. Those sources serve several purposes. Primarily, they demonstrate that scientists do not exist for themselves alone. At the same time, those accounts kindle enthusiasm in young minds, enrich those with an educated concern and entertain others with only a passing interest.

It is important to note, however, that recruitment and education must be legitimately promoted by scientists. Those expositions are not intended to be distracting or even instructive entertainment, although scientists are not interested in the man in the street only in so far as he may become a man in the laboratory. The enjoyment of apprehending and searching cannot be instilled by means of coercion and a sense of duty,[18] not even in the uninitiated. Authentic popular accounts of science are acceptable in so far as they limit themselves to a presentation of the subject avoiding wherever possible ulterior motives. As Einstein wrote many years ago, "science cannot create ends and, even less, instill them in human beings; science, at most, can supply the means by which to attain certain ends".[19]

Indeed, modern science would not have been born without a pre-reflective passionate striving for clear understanding. The personal commitment of the scientist teaches him that what his popular accounts of science do in the hands of the common man depends entirely on the nature of the goals alive in him.[20] He is content, therefore, to present his expositions in the language of the world and to let nature argue her own case, as it were. After all, if the scientist believes in such things as the rationality of the universe and the intuitive relation, surely he can be expected to try to live up to the promises of his scientific faith for the sake of mankind. Most of that small competent minority do. Einstein, for example, was firmly of the opinion that "the creations of our mind shall be a blessing and not a curse to mankind".[21] Einstein believed, of course, that the freedom of science meets the freedom of the person in the absence of all forms of coercion. Under those circumstances, science is free to choose the scientist, and *vice versa*. The chosen, however, are not elevated to exclusive privilege but to universal service.

Similarly, Christian faith is authentically proclaimed only if the word and work of the Person of Jesus Christ is allowed to declare itself through the ministry of the Holy Spirit. Proclamation in eloquent language, however, is not enough. It must be backed by the manner of living which prepares the theologian to apprehend God's love and concern for all mankind.[22] Such a way of life convinces him readily that men are able to learn more directly about the things of Christian living using the language of the world.[23] Christian thinking is not just to be learned within the confines of theological language or the Church. The Church exists for the world. It is the embodiment of the claim that Christian theology addresses effectually the problems and adversities of everyday life. That is why

Jesus sent his disciples into the world with its everyday language. But coercion is anathema to the Gospel of Jesus Christ. "It is not the mode of speaking, but the intentions of the heart and a godly conversation that recommend the faithful Christian."[24] The freedom of the Gospel must meet the freedom of the person if he is to choose God who has already chosen him.

It is obvious that the personal decisions of scientists and theologians have much common ground. The modes of communication in science and in theology are sufficiently similar to encourage the hope that their interface could be enlarged considerably. It would appear that, if goodwill is shown, there is sufficient ground for common endeavour without debilitating compromise. Certainly, they provide ample scope for an enriching empathy between the scientist and the theologian. Both are fully committed to service which demands the synergy of thought and action using technical language that must be translated to the benefit of all mankind.

NOTES

1. Athanasius, *Ad Episcopos*, 4.
2. *De Incarn.*, 27.2.
3. *Ibid.*, 57.1.
4. H. Bondi, *Assumption and Myth in Physical Theory*, Cambridge: Cambridge University Press, 1967, pp. 296f.
5. *Philosopher-Scientist*, p. 17.
6. Athanasius, *letter xix*, Easter 347.7.
7. *Isaiah*, 55.8.
8. *Ideas and Opinions*, pp. 261f.
9. *De Incarn.*, 42.6.
10. *C. Arianos*, i.37.
11. *Later Years*, p. 59.
12. *Evolution of Physics*, p. 13.
13. *Ideas and Opinions*, p. 324.
14. *Ibid.*, pp. 25f.
15. Athanasius, *Letter lii*.
16. A. Einstein, in Foreword to L. Barnett, *The Universe and Dr. Einstein*, New York: Bantam Books, 1968, p. 9.
17. *Ideas and Opinions*, p. 14.
18. *Philosopher-Scientist*, p. 17.
19. *Later Years*, p. 124.

20. *Ideas and Opinions*, p. 337.
21. *Philosopher-Scientist*, p. 650.
22. *De Incarn.*, 57.3.
23. *Ibid.*, 12.2.
24. *Ad Episcopos*, 9.

CHAPTER 5

THE UNIVERSE

OFTEN scientists speak of the universe and theologians refer to God in some remarkably similar ways. By faith, Christians apprehend that the world was made by the Word of God,[1] but that the bare notion of God transcends human thoughts.[2] The word God signifies the One who is different from things that are made and from all the creation. God illumines the world.[3] He is the almighty Deliverer from the shackles of man's illusions and imaginings.[4] This means that the Christian exodus cannot rest in anything or anyone other than him who is the Saviour. The Christian life involves seeking and searching along the way of and to God who is neither detected nor invented by men. Indeed, according to Christian teaching, the universe subsists in reason, wisdom and skill and is perfectly ordered throughout because God is over it and has ordered it as the Reason or Word of God.[5] Falsifying all alternative claims, God alone is the Truth. Yet, beyond all possible expectation, man meets the Reality whom he never found for himself or discovered by himself, the Reason who miraculously gifts him the abundant life.

By faith in an external world independent of the perceiving subject[6] and in the possibility that the regulations valid for the world of existence are rational,[7] modern science apprehends the world. But the object of scientific faith, the universe, transcends scientific theory. It cannot be comprehensively described or fully understood. As a complete entity, it can only be regarded quantitatively. Confronted by the great diversity of sense impressions, scientists begin by selecting those which lend themselves to order and meaning. Scientific explanations are inevitably inadequate and incomplete for the simple reason that science does not profess to deal with experience as a whole, but only with certain aspects of it in restricted contexts. The modern scientist does not claim that what is experienced as quantity is real and what is experienced as quality is an illusion. Scientific research is always subordinate to the given natural order of which current scientific apprehension is like a drop in the ocean. Moreover, many of its familiar quantitatively expressed details are actually reminders of the existence of the vast unexplored and unknown stretches of universal structure. They are intimations of "the eternally unattainable in the field of scientific endeavours".[8] Still, the reality of the universe provides the foundation for scientific activity, meaning and hope. The invariance of its pervasive rationality represents the matrix necessary for scientific experience, research and growth.

Like God, the universe is not a product of the scientific imagination. It cannot be lightly dismissed as an arbitrary invention of the human intellect. On the contrary, it is, so to speak, the great liberator which frees scientists from the fears of delusion and fantasy, and which guides them across the wastelands of manipulation. Just as God has called Christians not to the spirit of bondage to fear but to liberty,[9] so the practical pursuit of objective knowledge of the universe detaches scientists from self-centred passions and illusions. In fact, such a claim is not anathema to Christian faith. It is virtually embraced, for example, by the Athanasian declaration that "the Lord touched all parts of creation and freed and undeceived all of them from every illusion".[10]

Although modern science is characterised by seeking and searching, there is peace and security in the reality that the universe itself is neither invented nor discovered by scientists. By relying on the co-ordinative role of scientific concepts, scientists can submit to an independent reality in order to raise their thinking and doing above the "merely personal"[11] to the rational. Somewhat like its Creator, the universe excludes all other claims to authority and meaning as it directs scientists along its distinctive way.

God is by nature invisible and incomprehensible, having

his Being beyond all created existence.[12] God is above the feelings, strivings, derivations and motivations of the human being. His power far outreaches the littleness of images.[13] To insist that God is definable is to emulate the people of Israel when they preferred to erect temporal, visible, touchable idols of wood or stone rather than relate to eternal invisible God of Moses and the prophets. It is to favour a construction of the mind and to reject the reality that there can be no legitimate explanation of the inexplicable. God is real in the sense that God is unoriginate. Like the universe, God is a whole, but unlike the universe he is not a number of parts. He does not consist of diverse elements, but is himself the Maker of the system of the universe.[14] Consequently, God is manifest and made manifest to human persons only through himself. For man to feel, to think, to search and to find to the utmost of his abilities are not enough to disclose or to discover God. Man has fallen far short of being able to comprehend and know his Maker.[15] Nevertheless, God has chosen to make himself knowable to man. He has united himself to man in the Word incarnate who in his divine-human freedom is beyond the control or manipulation of man.

Likewise, the basic principles of modern science cannot be understood properly without the knowledge that the universe is the source of scientific freedom and wisdom. It is ultimately beyond the control and manipulation of man. As Einstein explained, "the contemplation of this world beckoned like a liberation, and I soon noticed that many a person whom I had learned to esteem and to admire had found inner freedom and security in devoted occupation with it".[16] Clearly, for Einstein, and indeed for the vast majority of scientists, scientific research involves confrontations with reality. Scientists are struck by thoughts as well as observations. Those encounters are primarily invitations extended by the universe which stands like a great eternal riddle only partially open to scientific thinking and current investigation.[17]

Scientists can respond freely, although the universe stretches out beyond their deepest intuitions and keenest

THE UNIVERSE

strivings. Similarly, theologians discourse with freedom of religious faith even as the good news of the Word incarnate surpasses the power of human telling.[18] Fundamentally, the universe is accessible and made accessible to scientists only by its own actions. It is beyond the realms of validity of the most general scientific theories. Host to the scientific enterprise which is only a little part of nature, the universe remains the undisputed master in its own house. It tolerates no rivals. As far as science is concerned, there is one universe which declares itself to be real and knowable and before which there can be no others.

Scientists are not at work to prove the existence of the world. This requires no proof for it is both active and determinate. The universe is apprehended in the natural order which intimates its existence. In Einstein's words, "the rational structure of an independent reality can be cognised by virtue of a pre-established harmony between thought and reality".[19] But the comprehensibility of the universe is inaccessible and its existence cannot be discovered by scientists. In its profoundest depths, the rationality of the universe is unsearchable.[20] Consequently, scientists speak of the world knowing that it cannot be successfully defined or adequately described. Rarely do scientists forget that they are looking into the kaleidoscope of sense experiences at a particular time and location on the boundary of the infinitely unknown.

"It is a fact that the totality of sense experiences is so constituted as to permit putting them in order by means of thinking — a fact which can only leave us astonished, but which we shall never comprehend. One can say: the eternally incomprehensible thing about the world is its apprehensibility".[21] Thus, scientists refer to the universe as the reality of a partially disclosed givenness which is inconceivable. In any case, if scientists cannot explain its knowability, how can they hope to define the universe? To grasp in scientific concepts the universe in its entirety is obviously impossible. This non-formal notion — excepting cosmology — is used, therefore, when scientists speak of a dynamically ordered, harmonious, creative entity which discloses itself to mankind. Yet, even limited knowledge of it is still knowledge of its existence, activity and order. In fact, modern science is the story of man's heuristic and reflective responses to the unfolding universe.

Christian theology starts from the teaching of both the Old and New Testaments.[22] The Bible speaks of the One of whom human nature cannot get any idea at all.[23] God, like the universe, cannot be grasped in human concepts. God is inconceivable. In the words of Athanasius, "God is invisible and inaccessible to originated things, and especially to men on earth".[24] Consequently, the God who is to be seen and heard in the Bible cannot be proved to exist. Like his world, God acts and in the work and word of the Person of Jesus Christ he proves that he is a living God who is unsearchable and undiscovered in his profoundest depths. God's deeds correspond to his nature, so that the actor is made known by his act, and the action is ascertainable from his nature.[25] Who can declare the Father by number, so as to discover the powers of his Word? Only he who is the Word. His deeds in history prove the existence of God. They describe his nature and being. The God who was hidden from mankind has revealed himself in Jesus Christ, and what was thought impossible by men, Jesus demonstrates as possible.[26]

But Athanasius widely cautioned that the achievements of the Word incarnate "are of such a kind and number, that if one should wish to enumerate them, he may be compared to men who gaze at the expanse of the sea and wish to count its waves. For as one cannot take in the whole of the waves with his eyes, for those which are coming on baffle the sense of him that attempts it; so for him that would take in all the achievements of Christ in the body, it is impossible to take in the whole, even by reckoning them up, as those which go beyond his thought are more than those he thinks he has taken in. Better is it, then, not to aim at speaking of the whole, where one cannot do justice even to a part ..."[27] Evidently, Athanasius and Einstein shared a common concern for humility in the pursuit of truth and wisdom.

Nevertheless, by the Word revealing himself in the whole of the creation, all things have been filled with the knowledge of God.[28] And knowledge of God is knowledge of his existence, life and revelation. A covenant was set up between God and man. God came as a little child, died on the Cross and redeemed man. God became visible in Jesus who is the only image of the Father and the unique way of reaching the concept of the Father.[29] There are no other gods. Jesus Christ is the image of the invisible God, the first-born of all creation; for in, through and for him all things were created, things visible and things invisible, and he is the Head of the Body, the Church.[30] Perceiving the Word of the Father, men are able through him to gain some conception of the Father, and knowing their Creator, to avoid fashioning for themselves one invention after another.[31] This covenant is grounded in Jesus Christ, the Reality in whom God lives, acts and makes himself known.

The Word incarnate corrected man's neglect by his own teaching, restoring all that was man's by his own power.[32] Consequently, no novelties and no abstractions must be made if the nature and existence of God are to be known.[33] Only God's work of grace and mercy opens up the reality that, in his covenant in Jesus Christ, men experience love and freedom. Without God, men fall from love and freedom into bondage and tyranny, into arbitrary inventions and chaotic illusions. But, if they are rooted and grounded in love, they may have power to apprehend what is the breadth and length and height and depth, and to know the love of Christ which surpasses knowledge. They may be filled with all the fullness of God.[34] However, in their thinking, theologians must be like Athanasius who was ever conscious of the vast ocean of God's love.

The rationality of the universe is, so to speak, the covenant between man and the world. For scientists, reality is invariant. A real world exists to be appreciated by scientific research. Inconceivably, the universe behaves as the world of man. It has established this covenant with man as the guarantee of the enrichment of his life in return for his commitment and obedience to the natural order.

Scientific thinking is, therefore, thinking of, and on the basis of, the given reality of the rational universe. Reflecting its Creator, the universe exists, acts, makes itself known as the reality which is this covenant. The objective laws of nature are determinate. Scientists exercise scientific freedom by humble dependence on the natural order. Amidst a variety of scientific theories, the unity of the natural order constrains scientists by its greater unobservable rationality as it intimates itself in the lesser observable phenomena.

No disembodied arbitrary abstractions must be made if the nature and existence of the universe are to be properly investigated. Scientific wisdom can only spring from the soil of experimental science,[35] from the comparisons of the inventions of the intellect with observed facts.[36] Scientific thinking is not impersonal or abstract but depends on the correlation of mind and matter. Ultimately, of course, abstraction is rejected by scientists on the basis of the conviction that the universe expounds itself. Scientific researchers, therefore, learn exclusively from it of the riches of scientific freedom and wisdom. This instruction is only gained on encountering and obeying the self-disclosing universe.

Obviously, scientific freedom must be structured in some way if it is to be meaningful. The ordering of its structure originates beyond the scientist in the universe itself. Without this freedom, scientific wisdom cannot be assimilated. Apart from this wisdom, scientific freedom is little different from all the other forms of intellectual slavery that have their bases in superstition. But, if scientists are firmly anchored and securely bound to the rationality of the universe, they may have power to understand the world and to know its rationality which outreaches all scientific theory. They may experience "a rapturous amazement at the harmony of the natural law".[37]

In brief, the bare notions of the universe and God transcend human thought. The scientific enterprise and the Christian life involve seeking and searching along the unique ways of the universe and the Word incarnate, respectively. Neither God nor the universe is invented or discovered by unaided human reason. God and the universe are real and make themselves knowable. In their distinctive ways, they can liberate the person from fear, illusion and manipulation while excluding all other claims to authority and meaning. There are no other gods or universes. Both God and the universe are unprovable, inconceivable and unsearchable in their profoundest depths. Nevertheless, even limited knowledge of God or of the universe is still knowledge of their existence, activity and self-disclosure. Whereas Christians experience love and freedom in God's covenant in Jesus Christ, scientists exercise wisdom and freedom by humble dependence on the rationality of the universe.

It would appear that there are sufficient common conceptual grounds to encourage the hope that those scientists who are anchored and bound to the rationality of the universe and those theologians who are grounded in the love of God will be capable of and inclined to a mutual understanding of the special powers that they have been freely given.

NOTES

1. *Hebrews*, 9v3.
2. *C. Arianos*, i.23.
3. *C. Gentes*, 40.4.
4. *Ibid.*, 7.5.
5. *Ibid.*, 40.3.
6. *Ideas and Opinions*, p. 266.
7. *Ideas and Opinions*, pp. 46f.
8. *Ibid.*, p. 9.
9. *Galations*, 5v13.
10. *De Incarn.*, 45.5.
11. *Philosopher-Scientist*, pp. 5f.
12. *C. Gentes*, 35.1.
13. *Ibid.*, 21.1.
14. *Ibid.*, 28.3.
15. *De Incarn.*, 11.1.
16. *Philosopher-Scientist*, pp. 5f.
17. *Ibid.*
18. *C. Arianos*, i.9.
19. *Ideas and Opinions*, p. 226.

20. *Ibid.*, p. 49.
21. *Later Years*, p. 61.
22. Athanasius, *Ad Adelphum*, 6.
23. *De Incarn.*, 11.1.
24. *C. Arianos*, i.63.
25. *C. Gentes*, 16.4.
26. *De Incarn.*, 1.2.
27. *Ibid.*, 54.4–5.
28. *Ibid.*, 16.1.
29. *C. Gentes*, 34.3.
30. *Colossians*, ivv15–8.
31. *De Incarn.*, 11.3.
32. *Ibid.*, 10.1.
33. Athanasius, *Ad Episcopos Ægypti*, 21.
34. *Ephesians*, 3.17–19.
35. H. Minkowski, in H. A. Lorentz *et al.*, *The Principle of Relativity*, translated by W. Perrett and G. B. Jeffrey, New York: Dover Publications, 1923, p. 75.
36. *Ideas and Opinions*, p. 266.
37. *Ibid.*, p. 40.

CHAPTER 6

UNIVERSAL UNITY

ANOTHER parallelism of the ways in which the natures of God and of the universe can be apprehended is now outlined. All scientific endeavour is pointless if the universe is not a unified whole, a unity. From an Einsteinian perspective, however, universal unity is not the same as arithmetical unity. In attempting to understand experience, scientists arrive at the assumption of the universe as a unified whole. But they claim no more than a non-formal notion of universal unity. This notion amounts to an object of faith which accounts for the observed regularities of nature. Every new discovery of the complexity of the microcosm or the macrocosm serves to fill in the outline of what has already been inferred about the universal unity.

Certainly, they acknowledge its arithmetical unity. Nevertheless, this does not exhaust the concept of the unity of the universe to which all arithmetical unities point through the multiplicity of its events and processes. Moreover, familiarity with things like the periodic table of chemical elements is sufficient to convince most practising scientists that science rejects the uncritical presupposition that an entity which exhibits arithmetical unity is thereby more intelligible than an object which exists as a complex of members or operations. The atom, the nucleus, the stars and space-time are only a few of the many equally poignant reminders of the limitations of arithmetical unity, concepts that, in fact, serve as indices or echoes of universal unity.

Similarly, Christian theological activity is groundless if God is not a unity. But from the biblical record of divine acts, it is clear that the unity of God is not a simple arithmetical unity.[1] As the theological mind seeks to apprehend the significance of these acts, a non-formal notion of divine unity assumes a more definite content whose validity depends on the fidelity with which the relations within the biblical record are ordered. In other words, theological reflection surveys the empirical evidence of the early Church and attempts to formulate who God is. Theological thought always centres in the birth, death, resurrection and ascension of Jesus Christ and the gift of the Holy Spirit. As it does so, it realises that, in seeking to express itself systematically, human language and concepts fall far short of the demands made upon them. Hence, it concludes that divine unity is not only an arithmetical unity, but an essentially mysterious unity to which the multiplicity of divine acts points.

To state that the universe is a unity is to believe that, in its profoundest depths, this is valid. Modern science does not assert that all things are only relative. Natural laws are determinate despite the reality that all observers do not experience the same effects. The private times and spaces of different observers do not exist in isolation. They all belong to a single objective space-time called the universe which is invariant. By distinguishing the variant from the invariant, scientists penetrate the dynamic structures of reality, that is, they relate to the universe as a unified whole. Consequently, the unity of the universe is not merely a label attached by scientists to indicate that they think they know all about unity and have transplanted this term. Such a stance would be inconsistent with the self-disclosure of the universe and with the intuitions of generations of scientists. When scientists describe the universe as a unity, they mean that it is the source of all unity.

Theologians believe that the good news of what God has done and is doing in this world points beyond itself to the One who is a unified whole, a unity. What they have to proclaim is empirically grounded in the multiplicity of the events of the Gospel. Their reflection is quite definitely a rational activity involving acceptance of the biblical record without wilful distortion, deliberate rationalisation, or the solving of problems as an end in itself. Yet, this activity requires the acknowledgement of both the divine unity and the three divine Persons.² The Holy Spirit is inseparable from the Son and the Son is inseparable from the Father.³

This rational problem cannot be easily explained away, nor should it be dismissed as some figment of the theological imagination. Its authenticity is readily shown by its ability to account for the observed and recorded evidence. There is no alternative, therefore, but to recognise that divine unity is the dynamic union of the three Persons, a unitary whole from which the creation and all its unities ultimately derive their meaning. The doctrine of the Trinity is a formal expression of this ultimate mystery. It is not a closed statement made to obscure an irrationality. On the contrary, it is an open declaration of Christian faith, a humble acknowledgement that God permits successive generations to glimpse both what their mentors apprehended and what can prepare their progeny for greater clarity and understanding.

The universe is a unified whole in the sense that the content of modern science is only a pale shadow of its unity. It is not that there can be a human conception of unity and then a special instance of universal unity. What scientists call unity is derived from universal unity which is the origin and seat of all scientific unities. Incidentally, the same relation applies to the rationality of the universe as the source of all rationality. Yet, the nature of this unity lies beyond apprehension. It exists as the comprehensive unity that unifies the plentitude of natural, including arithmetical, unities of scientific experience. Universal unity intimates itself through the intuitive relation in the lesser observable unities of the world and in doing so illumines their multiplicities. As Einstein and Infeld explained, "a complete solution (to the mystery of the universe) seems to recede as we advance".⁴

Like all other concepts, the non-formal notion of universal unity is continually under revision as more and more of reality is experienced and apprehended. As scientists stand open to the structured world, they abandon ambitions of final solutions to scientific problems and epistemological systems.⁵ Nevertheless, the basic features of this concept remain essentially unchanged and fundamentally heuristic. The universe is a unified whole with an internal multiplicity, the echoes of which reverberate throughout the length and breadth, the height and depth of modern science.

According to Einstein, universal unity presents itself to scientists in the three activities of the independent world, its rationality and its intuitive relation.[6] Each of these is only known by its actions. The three are equally distinct but interperficient in that the universe exists by virtue of their mutual conditioning. There is a continuity known as the universe and a multiplicity observed as existence, order and knowability. The way in which independent reality acts is governed by natural laws and by the pre-established harmony between thought and reality. This interperficiency reveals the triunity of the universe, a mysterious unity in trinity. It must be stated, however, that the grounds for believing in the universe, in the rationality of the universe and in the intuitive relation cannot be put into the form of a compelling argument from which there is no possibility of escape. But this need not unduly perturb those who realise that no belief about the nature of the world is intellectually compelling or demonstrative.

An external world without structure would be chaos. An independent structured world without intelligibility would be utterly inaccessible to the human mind. The independence of the universe is disclosed in its rationality and together they form the basis for the intuitive relation. The three activities of the universe are necessary to explain the totality of scientific experience, and scientists are faced, therefore, with the mystery of an interperficient universal unity. However, most scientists are like Einstein who was "satisfied with the mystery of the eternity of life and with the awareness and a glimpse of the marvellous structure of the existing world, together with the devoted striving to comprehend a portion, be it ever so tiny, of the Reason that manifests itself in nature".[7] Scientists recognise that they are surrounded by the mystery of an incomprehensible reality. There are many things which are acceptably clarified by science and, no doubt, there is a great deal in the existing world which is presently regarded as mysterious and which will eventually become tolerably clear. But, when account is taken of all that is already known and of all that is scientifically knowable, the mysterious depths of the universe remain essentially unfathomed. The scientist has little reason, in spite of the prodigious advances of modern science, to assume that he or any of his successors will fathom the universe once and for all. To be scientific is to acknowledge the darkness as well as the light. The scientist does not yield to the temptation to claim more than he knows without paying a costly price.

Interperficiency is somewhat similar to the technical term *perichoresis* used by theologians to denote the dynamic unity of the one divine Life of the three Persons of the Godhead. This unprovable correspondence between the creation and the Creator may appear to some Christians as verging on idolatry. But by his own Word, God gave the universe the order it has.[8] Moreover, knowledge of the unity of the Godhead as revealed in Jesus Christ is knowledge of the Creator from whom the unity of the universe has its existence. Just as the unities of the world reflect the unity of the universe, so the latter mirrors the unity of its Creator. The believing Christian, of course, humbly acknowledges that only by the grace of God can his eyes be opened through the Holy Spirit to see the significance of such a correspondence. In fact, neither the unity of God nor of the universe can be comprehended. But it does not follow that what cannot be understood is untrue. They are mysteries that cannot be ignored since they account for the recorded empirical evidence of Christian life and modern science. In a nutshell, each demands an act of faith.

For Christian theology, the one God is the Father, the Son and the Holy Spirit. If the Son is named, the Father is in the Son, and the Holy Spirit is in the Son.[9] These three Persons are not three gods. God is not tritheistic but monotheistic. God is not divisible.[10] There is one divine Nature.[11] Theology understands the Trinity as one God.[12]

All that is recorded and experienced of the three Persons cannot be separated from the one revelation of the one God. In speaking of God as the Father, the theologian refers to him as the Source and Origin of the Son who is distinct from the Father in his Person but identical with him in his Divinity. God the Father begets God the Son[13] and the Reality of God is complete in the third Person of the Holy Spirit[14] who proceeds from both the Father and the Son. God the Father declares to mankind his Fatherhood in the Son and together they are the Origin of the Holy Spirit through whom persons become children of God.[15]

In speaking of the universe, scientists of an Einsteinian persuasion are already committed to its rationality and to the intuitive relation. What is said of the external world independent of the perceiving subject, or of the rationality of this world, or of the intuitive relation refers to the one universe. It is not a static entity but a dynamic creative whole exhibiting an abundance of internal motions. It confronts scientists in that profusion through which they come to know the natural order.

For scientists, the universe is real, rational and self-disclosing, a whole in three activities. The independent world is the source of that activity known as its rationality. But their mysterious interrelation does not exhaust the nature of the universe. There is a third activity of the universe called the intuitive relation. All that the universe is to scientists, independent reality, the invariant laws of nature and self-disclosure, is the inconceivable wholeness of the universe. Because the universe is what it is, the intuitive relation allows them to share in its complex motions, to investigate the events and processes of the world. Science is just a little part of the natural order. Scientists co-operate with nature as motes dancing in the universal beam. They do so simply because nature requires it of them. They are chosen to be co-workers with the universe in its rationality through the intuitive relation. Scientific research is readily understood in this way.

Although this distributive analogy is not proof, it does

have the merit of demonstrating that modern science and Christian theology sometimes follow closely similar tracks in their search for a greater understanding of reality. At the very least, it shows that science is not without its irreducible mysteries, and that the mysteries of theology can be better appreciated, on occasions, in the light of scientific thinking. The unities of God and of the universe illustrate these points. It would be foolish, however, to claim much more from such a rudimentary comparison. Nevertheless, the indications are that a more thorough investigation will amply reward those scientists and theologians who are committed to open dialogue.

NOTES

1. *Ad Serap.*, 1.31.
2. *Ibid.*, 1.28.
3. *Ibid.*, 1.33.
4. *Evolution of Physics*, p. 4.
5. *Ideas and Opinions*, pp. 225f.
6. *Ibid.*, p. 262.
7. *Ibid.*, p. 11.
8. *C. Gentes*, 35.1.
9. *Ad Serap.*, 1.14.
10. *Ibid.*, 1.20.
11. *Ibid.*, 1.14.
12. *Ibid.*
13. *Ibid.*, 1.15.
14. *Ibid.*, 1.25.
15. *Ibid.*, 1.24.

Chapter 7

UNIVERSAL AUTHORITY

AUTHORITY seems to play somewhat similar roles in modern science and in Christian theology. On the one side, whatever scientists say of the universe, it can never be more than an indication of its nature. On the other side, as already noted, theological statements about God are essentially inadequate. Scientific theories do not circumscribe the natural order. Instead, they are limited by remaining subject to the ultimate authority of the universe. Likewise, all theological concepts owe obedience to the authority of the Word of God. At no stage in the development of science can universal authority be rigorously defined from a scientific appreciation of its manifestations. This authority is determined solely by what the universe is. Scientists can only speak non-formally of universal authority while theologians talk of God's authority in incomplete and open terms.

Most scientists tacitly acknowledge that the universe does what it does, is not answerable to science and has an authority second to none. For theologians, God is who he is, is accountable to no other and is the Authority of all other authorities. As far as modern science is concerned, all other forms of authority are conditioned and limited by universal authority which has no authentic rivals. Science is a search for an understanding of nature, not a striving for power over it.[1] This search is always too promising and too humbling to encourage delusions of mastery over nature. Besides, history shows that the subtlety of nature repeatedly frustrates human endeavours for its exploitation or control.

The Word incarnate is the *Alpha* and the *Omega* of the creation, but the universe has the first and last word in scientific research. It has unique authority, but that authority is inseparable from the universe itself. Nor is the authority of God separable from God himself. Indeed, the universe exposes for science the falsity of all abstract notions of authority. Such abstractions are as fundamentally opposed to the structure and harmony of the universe as they are to the nature and revelation of God. By setting themselves above either the rule of natural law or the reign of divine love, these pseudo-authorities deny themselves any basis in reality. Their roots are grounded in self-assertion and their branches hold the fruits of manipulation.

Many decades ago, Einstein emphasised that "science cannot create ends and, even less, instill them in human beings; science, at most, can supply the means by which to attain certain ends".[2] Such claims are valid simply because science obeys the natural order. Yet, it cannot apprehend the universe without, at the same time, opening up possibilities for contriving things that improve or devalue life. This includes the arbitrariness of abstract authority which, in its turn, bites the hand that feeds it. As the history of Christian doctrines shows, theology is vulnerable to similar abuses but it cannot progress without risking new heresies or old ones in new guises.

The authority of the universe resides in the power of natural law. The unity of the natural order exists amidst a variety of scientific theories. The interplay of non-eternal theories and invariant laws of nature enables scientists to discover and to move beyond the inadequacies of current achievements. These laws are contemporaneous with every scientific age. They represent the order that exists in the external world, and their rationality is the source of all that is meaningful to scientists. In them, the authority of the universe becomes visible and active as enriching and enlightening power. By them, the universe sets the limit of all that is possible, including chaotic abstractions.

But the claims that the universe makes upon scientists demand more than mere intellectual assent. They require personal scientific responses, committed reactions, to the events and processes of nature that come to them as authoritative. The obligation which lies upon all scientists is to pursue the truth and to surrender themselves to what they are given to apprehend. Scientists are citizens of the universe. They are, therefore, in no position to dictate its terms of government.

The authority of God is given in the Person of the Word incarnate who came not to abolish but to fulfil the law of God.[3] Hence, it confronts mankind as the power of love in Jesus Christ who obeys the law of God. The power of love is, therefore, the ordering power that unifies the creation. There is one Lord Jesus Christ but a multiplicity of doctrinal interpretations. In the light of God's authority as the eternal Word, theologians can recognise and counteract distortions in their temporal theological systems. Thus they can modulate the prevailing winds of theological change. This Word is contemporaneous with every age. In him, theologians find all that is redemptive and rational. The authority of God is revealed and activated in the Word as enlivening power. He establishes all that is real and possible. He exposes all that is imaginary and impossible. In his birth, death, resurrection and ascension, he commands authoritatively the personal commitment of theologians who are granted citizenship of the Kingdom of God.

The Word incarnate declares to mankind that God is the Creator of the universe. He demonstrates that God is not dependent upon the thoughts of men. His life shows that the thoughts of men are not the thoughts of God. The reality of God is to be seen in Jesus Christ who, unpredictably and inconceivably, opened up the way of and to God. Theological activity starts and ends with God the Father, the Son and the Holy Spirit. And with this awareness, the profound mystery is seen to be the New Covenant in the body and blood of Jesus Christ.

The fact that theology is part of the work of the people of God, that it has a legitimate function within the life of the Church, emerges from the rule of love in the Servant-Lord. The Lord commands the free exercise of all human gifts for the glory of God. Christian freedom, therefore, derives its reality from the Word incarnate. It is freely gifted but mercifully limited by Jesus Christ who, himself, has been given full authority in heaven and on earth.[4] All Christian freedom is, therefore, a pale shadow of God's freedom in the Word incarnate. In fact, theologians are only free because the Son of God grants them the freedom to choose to obey the New Covenant and its law of love. Of course, they can always reject the authority of Jesus Christ in favour of self-assertion and its consequent chaos.

The universe intimates authoritatively that there is a reality distinct from the thoughts of scientists. It is recognisable in its rationality. Reality is open to scientists in the natural order, and, astonishingly, that openness is the intuitive relation. According to Einstein, scientists begin with the external world, its rationality and the intuitive relation. And from that standpoint, the great riddle is the intelligibility of the world, the fact that science is possible. The universe originates the scientific enterprise as part of its coinherent dynamics. Consequently, scientific freedom does not possess its reality of itself. It is established and limited by its subjection to natural law which prevails universally and intelligibly. All scientific freedom is only a weak reflection of universal freedom. Scientists are free by virtue of the superior freedom of the universe. Their freedom to choose is given by the universe. It is the freedom to decide for obedience to its order. Should scientists choose to abuse this freedom, they opt deliberately for power-sapping speculation, expediency and manipulation. By doing so they turn their backs on the authority of the universe and, therefore, depart from the scientific way.

Perhaps surprising to many non-scientists, modern science rejects as false the authority of a definitive world-view. Only those who either lack the time or inclination to examine the contents of modern science can accept the world-views inferred by the theories of science as complete and exhaustive accounts of reality. A little thought shows up the limitations of scientific theories. The law of gravity, for example, states that there is an attraction between the stone and the earth. Admittedly it gives a more precise description of the stone falling to the ground when dropped. It communicates in terms of an attractive force which depends on the masses of the stone and the earth and their distance apart. But, although something is said of how the stone falls, nothing is revealed of the mystery of why the stone falls or of why there is a law of gravity. Modern science never explains why things are as they are. It confines its attentions to the things that are.

In the course of the centuries, mankind has passed through several world-views, none of which adequately expressed the content of the contemporaneous science. Modern science is essentially free in regard to all world-views. It resists successfully, sooner or later, all attempts to restrict visions of reality by limited world-views based on incomplete and uncertain scientific theories.

Likewise, theologians realise that all expressions of the reality of God must sound like inchoate mumblings to the Word incarnate. Yet, they do not need to rely on their own resources to construct or to assimilate general views of the world. Jesus Christ has the authority to release them from the temporal conceptual restrictions of world-views. Christian theology cannot serve two masters. It must not, therefore, become the servant of any world-view, past or present. Theological language may reflect something of a particular world-view, but that does not mean that it acknowledges the authority of that world-view. In fact, the sacred and inspired Scriptures make many references to the ancient Near Eastern picture of the world without being confined by its conceptual limitations.

Einstein recognised that throughout science's history certain concepts that have proved useful in the constitution of an order of things readily win such an authority over some scientists that they tend to forget their origins and regard them as changeless data.[5] Theology's history tells a remarkably similar tale. A general lesson of history seems to be that history's lessons are seldom learned. However, less inhibited scientists or theologians insist on analysing current notions and investigating their justification and their empirical grounds. In this way, their exaggerated authority is exposed and their deficiencies uncovered. Without this relentless pursuit of truth, the logical ordering of empirical data crystallises as a rigid system, perhaps even as a definitive world-view. Inevitably, it tries to rival the authority of the universe or Jesus Christ, as the case may be. Obviously, scientific research and theological activity do not progress under those circumstances. At most, existing methods and concepts are entrenched. But obedience to the authority of the universe or Jesus Christ frees scientists or theologians, respectively, from the fear and futility of attempting to form a world-view of reality by relying on themselves.

From Einstein's outline of scientific thinking, it appears that the scientific mind depends heavily on topological thinking. It seems to do so not only in communicating knowledge but in apprehending reality. If this is a valid representation, it offers further resistance to the notion of a world-view in scientific thinking. All scientific theories are like signposts along the way of greater precision and fuller apprehension.[6] On the one hand, they combine faith with understanding. On the other hand, they surpass logical thought but are vulnerable to distortion by extraneous psychological factors. Briefly, scientific theories are indispensable but fallible. Significantly, there are no scientific theories of the unique and natural events and processes are correlated in ways that are not comprehensively reducible to common definable characteristics. These restrictions are hardly consistent with the holding of a definitive world-view.

Einstein placed great emphasis on the ordering and the surveying of sense impressions. This conceptual activity involves a pre-articulate phase which depends on creativity to bring order out of their lack of logical unity.[7] It is clear that a scientific concept does more than define common properties in a complex of particular instances. Actually, it is more like a member of a set of conceptual functions directing understanding beyond that set to its invariants as its basis in reality. It seems that Einstein explained the formation of concepts in simple topological terms.

Topological thinking applies the same theory in several different empirical contexts demonstrating its flexibility to serve beyond its original setting. According to Einstein, scientists have to deal not only with precise analysis and mathematical expression but also with personal participation which defies description. Hence, the objectivity of scientific theories can only reside in the invariance of the natural order, that is, in regions beyond the compass of any world-view. The relevant point is that the meanings of successive theories are topologically related by recurrent references to the increasing empirical surveys. Indeed, this is the only hope of eliminating extraneous psychological elements.

From an Einsteinian perspective, topological thinking makes possible the apprehension of what is not understood on the basis of what is understood. It achieves this simply because it relies on both empirical data and hidden conceptual connectivities. It is justified by the reliability with which its application orders and surveys new ranges of scientific data. Its only valid contact with reality comes from the universe which alone originates natural events and processes. The latter are beyond the scientist's intellectual abilities to create or to anticipate. Scientists can only reproduce and predict them. In their givenness, they are free from psychological distortion and, therefore, function as objective references in the development of scientific concepts and theories. The universal rationality to which they testify is the ground of all topological or scientific thinking which is, by nature, opposed to the formation of world-views.

Topological thinking also appears to give authentic expression to Christian theology. The Ten Commandments serve as guidelines directing human behaviour towards the constancy of God's love. The sayings of Jesus of Nazareth point through aspects of everyday living to the spiritual qualities of life. The pedagogic value of topological thought in communicating the good news of God in

Jesus Christ cannot be seriously called in question. Besides, theological activity always represents the attempt to understand more fully the deep things of Christian faith. At least to the open scientific mind, theology often appears to employ topological thinking in order to exceed logical restraints.

Surely, for example, to describe the Church as the Body of Christ or as the Bride of Christ is to speak topologically. Moreover, the theologian is encouraged to look beyond these two images to their common basis in God's love for mankind. In fact, their use forces theologians to ascribe a meaning to the Church which transcends their sum. If there is a legitimate place for topological thinking in Christian theology, there can be no room for a Christian world-view since they are mutually exclusive. Certainly, the role of topological thinking in theology deserves considerable attention in view of the current popularity of demythologism.

As scientists and theologians stand midway between the microcosm and the macrocosm, they inhabit the boundary between the known and the unknown. They can sense this environment and apprehend it. Faced with the inaudible, invisible and inarticulate, scientists realise that they cannot control the universe, while theologians acknowledge Jesus Christ as Lord. Indeed, scientific theories and experiments rely on universal authority but the validity of theological systems resides in the Word of God.

The flexile nexus of the conceivable and the inconceivable is characteristic of both scientific research and theological activity. It appears as a sign of the authority of the universe in every scientific concept, theory and experiment, in each scientific experience. This nexus reminds scientists that, although universal authority lies beyond the current limitations of science, its existence is still indicated within the events and processes of the natural order. Likewise, the variable boundary occurs as the hallmark of the authority of Jesus Christ on every theological concept, doctrine and system, on each theological experience. It sensitises theologians to the miracle that, although the authority of the Word incarnate surpasses temporal theological systems, that authority is revealed in the birth, death, resurrection and ascension of the Lord Jesus Christ. Clearly, Christian theology and modern science have much more in common than meets the eye.

NOTES

1. A. M. Taylor, *Imagination and The Growth of Science*, New York: Schocken Books, 1967, pp. 2f.
2. *Evolution of Physics*, pp. 151f.
3. *Matthew*, 5.17.
4. *Ibid.*, 28.18.
5. A. Einstein, quoted by M. Born in *Philosopher-Scientist*, p. 196.
6. *Ideas and Opinions*, p. 284.
7. *Later Years*, p. 63.

CHAPTER 8

THE RATIONALITY OF THE UNIVERSE

IN many respects the rationality of the universe is to scientists what Jesus Christ is to theologians. it must be abundantly clear from the preceding sections that any discussion of modern science or independent reality must inevitably make some reference to the rationality of the universe. In parallel, the centrality of the Word incarnate is indicated by all outlines of Christian theology and of God the Creator. Obviously, to talk scientifically of the universe is to work on the basis of its rationality and to presuppose the pre-established harmony between thought and reality. Similarly, to speak theologically of God is to communicate on the ground of the Word incarnate. This rationality represents the heart of science whereas the Word is the centre of theological activity. But universal rationality is not the product of scientific deliberation nor is the Word an utterance of man. The former belongs necessarily to the universe and the latter comes uniquely from God. The rationality of the universe and the Person of Jesus Christ are unique to science and theology, respectively. Not only does this rationality spring from the external world and issue in the intuitive relation, it illumines both of them. It resembles the Word incarnate who came from God the Father, who sent the Holy Spirit and in whom the other two Persons are seen.

Imagine the one-dimensional world of a hypothetical observer who had to describe the behaviour of a circle passing through his world. This individual sees the circle as a series of pairs of points, widening outwards from a central point and then contracting again. He knows about points, but this particular pattern of behaviour is new and puzzling. It suggests something beyond his immediate apprehension, the existence of a second dimension and the phenomenon of a circle.

So scientists perceive the rationality of the universe as its phenomena pass through their experience, freely and invariantly announcing the universe to them. The vast nexus of natural processes indicates that there is a universal order which comes to them through, although it lies beyond, their experiences. Consequently, scientists are a group of people deeply convinced that the rationality of the universe is the inclusive utterance of the universe in which they discover the meaning and justification of their activities. This is the thrilling adventure called modern science, an enterprise which historians, philosophers and theologians cannot convincingly explain away. The central enigma of modern science is a community of believers in the uniqueness of the rationality of the universe, a uniqueness that rests as much on what is thought as what is done.

Fundamental to modern science is the wonder that the universe is intelligible.[1] The corresponding miracle of Christian theology is that the Son of God became flesh and dwelt among men. All scientific theories, all scientific statements about the universe and the intuitive relation, can only amount to an extuberant expression of the natural order. The theological correlate is that all valid systematic theologies are necessarily expanding expositions of the nature of God. The uniqueness of the rationality of the universe and of the Person of Jesus Christ are essentially inclusive, not primarily exclusive. Consequently, wherever scientists or theologians attempt to theorise abstractly, they are trapped sooner or later in their own contradictions. The chemistry of the so-called inert gases and the Arian heresy are well-known examples. The same thing occurs either when scientists try to explain scientific researches exclusively in terms of illogical leaps or chance discoveries, or when theologians attempt to base expositions solely on subjective experiences. Then science or theology is apparently reduced to a sophisticated form of anarchy and the continuous development of science or theology is ignored in favour of methodological discontinuities or technical innovations, respectively.[2]

Actually the intuitive relation, like the Holy Spirit, is responsible for much more than sporadic flashes of insight. The Holy Spirit inspires all that Jesus Christ is to Christians and the intuitive relation inosculates, so to speak, all that the rationality of the universe means to scientists. Beginning with this rationality, scientists apprehend the pervasive harmony of nature to which they refer in amazement, yet about which they, like Einstein, can say relatively little.[3] In Jesus Christ alone theologians can see the miracle of the New Covenant between God and man, the communion that surpasses description. Only the rationality of the universe encompasses the natural order. Uniquely, the Word incarnate is the light of the world. Consequently, the theologian accepts Jesus Christ as Lord and the Holy Spirit as the Interpreter, and the scientist, being an iota of nature, acknowledges gratefully that the intuitive relation explicates this rationality.[4] For the scientist, all knowledge of reality begins and ends in experience of the rationality of the universe.[5] The relation between the truth of the universe and the truth-content of scientific theories is discernible and discerned in the light of this rationality,[6] just as the Truth of God for man is Jesus Christ.

The nave of science is the rationality of action and the action of rationality, and the hub of theology is the word of the Life and the life of the Word. The everyday distinction between thinking and doing, therefore, disappears in both science and theology. Theological activity and active theology are the two sides of the one coin. Theoretical science and experimental science are like two different craftsmen working on the same cathedral. This is why Einstein referred collectively to the theories, concepts and methods of science as the "deeds" of scientists.[7]

A commitment to scientific research or a life of Christian service is the basis for a growing apprehension of the universe or God, respectively. Throughout his life, Jesus of Nazareth remained faithful to the practices of Judaism. Consequently, he exposed the idolatry, legalism and hypocrisy of the political and religious leaders of his day. His challenge to authority and his fulfilment of the Law of God went hand in glove. In his person, creativity and criticism were inseparable. He criticised the traditions and conventions of his time by serving his fellow human beings. Jesus conflicted with the established sects and cults in his concern for others, and finally, in his life of service, he paid the ultimate price of commitment.

The life and work of Einstein illustrate that exacting service is required of the scientific researcher. Einstein tackled courageously fundamental problems associated with established theories. He was not diverted by the differing interpretations of his peers from what he saw as the main problems. Einstein challenged directly traditions with his extraordinary capacity to research. Yet, his scientific contributions are characterised by an unqualified obedience to the established scientific methods. His theories of relativity, his search for the elusive unified field theory and his running conflict with the available expositions of quantum theory were all based on extensive and intensive self-giving research. In fact, Einstein paid a very high price for his criticisms of old and new scientific conventions, and he did so knowingly and willingly.

What is involved in scientific research and in theological activity is the pursuit of truth and the truth of pursuit. The rationality of the universe acts, declares itself, and scientists react to its illumination of the external world. The Word incarnate lives, reveals himself and theologians respond to the revelation of God the Father.

All that is properly called scientific or theological knowledge is knowledge of this rationality or the Word, respectively. Universal rationality confronts scientists with the mystery that the universe has an ordered content which is largely unexplored and inaccessible,[8] while the Word incarnate beckons theologians to believe that God identifies himself in human flesh, that he who is inconceivable and unapproachable was made man. Theologians or scientists stand humbled before the Word or nature as they receive intimations of reality. On the one hand, this rationality dwarfs scientific knowledge[9] and, on the other hand, it invites scientific investigation.[10] On the one side, the Word exposes the frailty of human reasoning and, on the other, he commands the adventure of love. He does so by approaching man as a fellow creature in history. Similarly, this rationality alone explains the totality of the universe while reaching out to scientists in the multiplicity of natural events and processes. It is, so to speak, the reality of the covenant between the universe and man, just as Jesus Christ is the Reality of the New Covenant between God and man.

When scientists recognise novel aspects of the former covenant, they are empowered to theorise anew about independent reality. As theologians participate in the New Covenant, they are enlivened to articulate freshly the love of God the Father. In the Word incarnate they meet the concrete form of God, and in this rationality scientists are able to apprehend the real structure of the universe. Scientists of an Einsteinian persuasion are encouraged in the fact of this covenant to speak of the intuitive relation by which the universe inspires and guides them. Moreover, this guidance cannot possibly be an accident since it conforms to the laws of nature that exhibit invariance across the entirety of space-time. In view of the New Covenant, theologians talk confidently of the reality of the Holy Spirit who counsels and comforts them as they venture in faith to meet the challenges of their generation.

For theologians, there is no other God than the God who revealed himself in the birth, death, resurrection and ascension of Jesus Christ. In thinking theologically Christians begin with Jesus the Christ, the unity of God and man, who is the Truth. God embraces persons in Jesus Christ who immerses them in the truth and love of God. There is no place to hide from this sustaining love which can liberate persons from the bondage of sin. Theological systems cannot, of course, capture the Truth but they can be grasped by him. In so far as they echo the Truth, they proclaim freedom from the slavery of building conceptual pyramids. And in pointing beyond themselves, they resemble the Truth for he witnesses not to himself but to God the Father from whom he came, and to God the Holy Spirit who proceeds from both the Father and the Son. To adapt Athanasian terms, God the Father, the Son and the Holy Spirit are the Source, the Radiation and the Action of the light of Truth or Rationality. Theological activity is essentially a journey in pursuit of the Truth. Like Abraham, theologians depart in faith from familiar conceptual ground for unknown destinations. *En route*, they enjoy the privilege of the guidance of the Spirit of Truth as they follow the Way of Truth to the Source of Truth.

From an Einsteinian standpoint, there is no other universe than the one that is disclosed in rational action and active rationality. In thinking scientifically, scientists have from the beginning to think of the rationality of the universe. The unity of the universe and the scientist, this covenant, is inescapable. It envelops him in its rationality which promises his release from delusion, fantasy and contrivance. Granted that his theories are somewhat remote from this rationality,[11] they are nevertheless faint reflections of that rationality and as such they promote liberation from illusion.[12] Simultaneously, this rationality points to independent reality as its origin and to the operation of the intuitive relation as its consequence. The universe is, as it were, the sourcebook of rationality and the intuitive relation is the tutor who takes scientists through the course. They find themselves reading this course in faith and their personal progress gives them specific views of the structured world.[13] In short, this rationality sets the stage for the performances of modern science.

According to scientific faith, this rationality is the unique decisive disclosure of the external world. As already noted, it is the book of nature written by the universe with binding authority on scientists. They are influenced by many other factors, even intoxicated from time to time by their own theories, but nothing has the power of this rationality in science. Only it can free them from all lesser authorities that abandon them before the savagery of ambiguity or relativism. It confers on valid scientific theories the status of ambassadors. As scientists experience more and more of the natural order, they dispense with their extrinsic convictions, enthusiasms and preferences because of their deepening commitment to the objectivity of the structured world. Clearly, when they talk of this rationality, they refer to that supreme power which is the disclosure of the universe.

The reality of which scientists speak, this disclosure in rationality, is exclusive and authoritative. Scientists are concerned with nothing less than that reality which is the universe itself. Its rationality is distinguished by them as compelling and objective. In its rationality, the universe challenges scientists to use their inferior powers of logic and rationality to apprehend its manifestations. Confronted by the unfathomable depths of this rationality, they accept this challenge to investigate and to abide by the invariant laws of nature. Characteristically, every scientific theory, statement or concept has an objective content associated with this rationality. In other words, modern science rises above mere opinion in so far as it acts and communicates on the basis of the natural order.

God's revelation in Jesus Christ is the singular comprehensive Message who proceeds from God the Father. This proclamation is none other than the eternal Word expressed uniquely and authoritatively in human flesh. The labours of theologians can be affected by a whole variety of pressures including self-satisfaction with their own systematisations. Yet, all of them lack the real authority to direct activity beyond themselves. Sooner or later, theologians realise that they are caught by the force of a narrow whirlpool of subjective conceptualisation. Only Jesus Christ has the power to free them from provisional systems and ambivalent enthusiasms by binding them to the objective, conclusive, personal Word of God. The Word incarnate is the touchstone of all theological activity. As theologians grow in a knowledge, love and grace of the Lord Jesus Christ, they abandon progressively their subordinal baggage preferring the primary objective, economic authority of the Person of the Word. They acknowledge and adore the sovereign Power who is above all powers, the Word incarnate.

Since God's revelation in Jesus Christ is the work and word of the Person of the Son of God, theologians know that God himself is involved exclusively and authoritatively. The Word is uniquely the Reality of God disclosed in and to man personally and, therefore, objectively. In the Word incarnate, God invites persons to use their capabilities and propensities to understand, even as they live by, the New Covenant. Faced with the abundance of the life of the Word, theologians try to abide by the new commandment of love. They seek to apprehend more fully the good news of God in Jesus Christ. This is the only way to ensure that theological systems, statements and concepts have an objective content originating in the Word himself. In short, theological activity leaves the subjective behind in so far as it works for and witnesses to the Person of Jesus Christ.

Jesus Christ is the Lord. This means that Christians belong to him. In particular, it commands that theologians serve him in all that they try to accomplish. As just noted, they are freed from the fears of subjectivism into the hope of objectivity. This is the correct word because the Word incarnate is concerned about all persons whether they know it or not. Each person must decide how to respond to Jesus the Christ who is the *Alpha* and the *Omega*. Clearly, Christian faith is the decision to acknowledge Jesus Christ as Lord, to recognise his sovereign authority over one's life and over all the creation. Yet, the power of the Lord Jesus is not a blind force over Christians. This power orders the whole creation and, therefore, in the Word incarnate human wisdom attains supreme order or wisdom. This objective order is established apart from theologians who must subject themselves to it for it alone imbues all theological activity with real content.

In an important sense, the rationality of the universe claims scientists as its own. Scientific researchers obey it in all that they seek to do. In return, they escape from subjective life to the world of objective perception and

RATIONALITY OF THE UNIVERSE 81

thought.[14] But the matter does not end there. The existence of a rational universe has consequences for all men whether they realise it or not. Because this rationality is and was and will be within space-time, men may decide how they will react to its existence. Scientific faith is the decision to acknowledge the authority of this rationality. The value of this rationality is its power over scientists, not a power for power's sake, but the ordering power of scientific wisdom. An objective order exists apart from scientists, an order to which scientists must be submissive, an order which represents the concrete coherence of all scientific thought and action.

Scientists are children of the universe, people who believe that they contribute to the harmony of the world. Their activity within the natural order is objectively established. Primarily, there is no morality involved but, since scientists are given the freedom to research, morality plays a necessary but secondary role.[15] The scientific community is held together by obedience to the rationality of the universe. That obedience requires personal decisions. However, before *homo sapiens* appeared or apprehended it, the power of this rationality prepared the ground for him. This preparation includes the scientist's deliverance from bondage to all other powers. It energises the scientific community. Yet, the truth of this rationality does not depend on the formation of such a community or its recognition of this truth.

Knowledge of this truth occurs as the rationality of the universe places scientists at turning points in the history of the human intellect.[16] They are called personally to serve in "the temple of science",[17] that is, to serve this rationality and to communicate their understanding of it, perhaps even to the world at large. If science is to be obedient to this rationality, it must exist for the sake of mankind. What it discovers it must pass on through skilled interpreters within the scientific community. By doing this, it avoids setting itself up as a rival authority to the rationality of the universe and it reduces the risk of raising false hopes for scientific faith and wisdom. Scientists are not in business to convert the whole human race to scientific ways of thinking and doing, but they are prepared to share the experiences that enrich their lives. They are willing to point to that rationality which has the power to give them such freedom of inquiry.

Christians are followers of Jesus Christ, the adopted children of God the Father, who believe that they have a message of salvation to proclaim to the world. Their mission within the world is objectively grounded in the Word incarnate. Moral considerations flow from the freedom persons find in the Lord Jesus Christ. They are not prior to this sense of belonging, but result inevitably from it. The Body of Jesus Christ, the Church, is held together by obedience to their Lord. Obedience requires personal decisions, and schisms occur where disobedience reigns.

The power of the Word incarnate, however, cannot be diminished. He laid the foundation of the Church and exposed the inadequacy of all other powers. Jesus Christ unifies his followers as the company of believers although he does not need the worship or recognition of this fellowship. Knowledge of him who is the Truth comes as God elects Christians to serve their Lord in their day, generation and location within his Church. Theologians are personally called to increase understanding of the Reality of God and to communicate it to the Church and the world. Yet, they are not commissioned to convert the whole Church to theological thinking and language. They labour to explicate humbly the deep things of Christian faith that point beyond all human endeavours to the Word incarnate who gifts to all persons true freedom of inquiry.

Apparently, the function of the rationality of the universe in science is like a pale reflection of the work and word of the Person of Jesus Christ in theology. The similarity is, of course, strictly limited since there is no interpersonal bond between the universe and man that corresponds to the communion of God and man. Nevertheless, a fairly extensive correlation is readily sketched and it cannot be lightly dismissed by scientists or theologians without disparaging their own disciplines. Those common foun-

RATIONALITY OF THE UNIVERSE

dations, if not origins, seem to hold the key to much more detailed investigations that promise a better understanding between scientist and theologian.

NOTES

1. *Later Years*, p. 61.
2. *Thematic Origins*, p. 116.
3. *Ideas and Opinions*, p. 49.
4. *Ibid.*, p. 226.
5. A. Einstein, quoted in *A Centenary Volume*, p. 113.
6. *Philosopher-Scientist*, p. 13.
7. A. Einstein, quoted in *A Centenary Volume*, p. 113.
8. *Ideas and Opinions*, p. 49.
9. *Ibid.*, p. 40.
10. *Later Years*, p. 64.
11. *Evolution of Physics*, p. 10.
12. *Philosopher-Scientist*, pp. 5f.
13. A. Einstein, quoted in *A Centenary Volume*, p. 245.
14. *Ideas and Opinions*, pp. 225f.
15. G. Holton, *The Scientific Imagination: Case Studies*, London, New York and Melbourne: Cambridge University Press, 1978, pp. 245 and 248.
16. *Ideas and Opinions*, p. 254.
17. *Ibid*, p. 224.

Chapter 9

THE INTUITIVE RELATION

WHEREAS Christians believe in the Holy Spirit, scientists of an Einsteinian persuasion believe in the intuitive relation. While theologians understand God the Father as referring to God in his ultimate ineffability and God the Son as referring to his unique self-communication, they think of God the Holy Spirit as referring to God indwelling and enlightening man. In parallel, scientists look upon the external world, the rationality of the universe and the intuitive relation as independent reality, its comprehensively ordered nature and its relevance for scientists. As already discussed, the three activities of God or of the universe are inseparable being properly understood only in their unities. It must be noted, of course, that there are Christians to whom God the Father means something, and to whom Jesus Christ means something, but to whom the Holy Spirit means very little. Likewise, there are scientists to whom the universe is a reality, and to whom the rationality of the universe is meaningful, but to whom the intuitive relation is practically unknown.

Nevertheless, the intuitive relation specifically reminds scientists that they are actively immersed in the dynamics of the universe, that they belong to the universe. While scientists may try to think independently of the universe and to be the centre of their own work, the intuitive relation seldom lets them rest on their laurels for too long. Correspondingly, the Holy Spirit convinces theologians that they participate in the work of God, that they are co-workers with God. Scientists or theologians have faith in objective rationality, a faith that is exercised and, therefore, deepened as they investigate the wonders and ways of nature or of God. That scientific research is possible is due primarily to the existence of the intuitive relation, the mysterious vanguard of the universe. Christian theology is essentially and ineffably dependent on the Person of the Holy Spirit.

Theological activity is a necessary but partial response of the Church to Jesus Christ who came to fulfil the law of God. Jesus was born for mankind. He lived, died and rose again for the whole of humanity. Whether or not men acknowledge it, Jesus Christ is the Word incarnate. By him all things were made. Every man owes his existence to the eternal Word although each person must decide for himself how he will relate to the creative objective Rationality who is the Son of God. Persons who believe and live in Christ and who have freely committed themselves to systematic expositions of the work and word of the Person of Jesus Christ are called theologians. Through the Holy Spirit, they experience the confidence and hope that spring from creative Reality and the joy and peace that radiate from objective Reason.

Similarly, scientific research is man's commitment to the laws of nature. Scientists share this common basis in so far as they depend on the structures and regularities of nature. This dependency remains blind or superstitious, however, until they recognise and relate to the all-embracing rationality which releases them from the terrors of caprice. The individual left to himself is subject to a welter of conflicting impulses. But persons who believe in this comprehensive rationality and who are liberated from fear to investigate and to apprehend its manifestations are called scientific researchers. Through the intuitive relation, they are free to enjoy the peace and security of objective reality, privileged to experience the flight of ignorance and superstition.[1]

Not all persons are scientists, and not all scientists are physicists. Scientific freedom seems to come as a distinct gift of the universe to the person.[2] While such a gift must be developed, it cannot be achieved by human capacities or strivings. Indeed, nothing can be said concerning the exact nature of this freedom or of the relation between the rationality of the universe and the scientist beyond the assertion that the intuitive relation is the *inconceivable movement from this rationality to man*. Scientists are those who are receptive and also responsive to this infusion. All else about this relation remains hidden in the mystery of the universe. Its existence is known only through its consequences, that is, through the involvement of scientists in the events and processes of the universe.[3]

The claim is effectively that scientists are inspired in a special way, that through the obedience of their wills and minds, their working lives, the universe speaks. This does not mean that the universe communicates in the form of infallible propositions and, therefore, that scientific knowledge is exempt from error being deducible from a set of disclosed premises. On the contrary, the universe mysteriously impinges on scientists who must seek to interpret its way. Through the intuitive relation the universe cooperates with scientists in their discovering. The intuitive relation is not merely a source of invigoration, a releasing of the person's natural energies. It involves an experience that carries the person out from his individual isolation into the common fields of scientific endeavour. The inspiration of individuals is a consequence of, and subordinate to, the corporate scientific enterprise. By responding personally to the rationality of the universe through the intuitive relation, individuals act as citizens of the universe in the special sense that they obey its orders and acknowledge its work as their own. They become scientists, the standard-bearers of its rationality.

It is equally apparent that not all persons are Christians. Followers of Jesus Christ have mysteriously received the gift of the Holy Spirit. This gift gives them the freedom to apprehend the word and work of Jesus Christ and to live as the children of God. Where the Spirit of the Lord is, there is a movement of God toward man which precedes and enables a movement of man toward God. Jesus Christ breathes his Spirit upon persons empowering them to proclaim the message of his Church. In particular, theologians are enlivened to explicate the deep things of the Christian faith. While the indwelling Holy Spirit is a mystery to man, a miracle wrought by the love of God in Jesus Christ, this human experience engages the will and the mind, in fact, the complete person. Yet, Christians do not possess the Holy Spirit. On the contrary, they are the bearers of the good news of God, of the Word incarnate, in so far as they are obedient to the promptings and guidance of the Holy Spirit. Where persons are attentive and responsive to the guidance of the Holy Spirit, they acknowledge that they are only at the beginning of understanding the comprehensive works of God.

An openness to the Word incarnate is the God-given freedom that theologians nurture as they receive the counsel of the Holy Spirit. This means that they can relate validly to the sacred and inspired Scriptures as they systematise the proclamation of the Gospel. They are acutely aware of the wonder that, if they grasp after Christian freedom, they will chase it away, but that, if they are to be caught up by this freedom, they must put self-assertion to flight. A personal relationship with Jesus Christ through the Spirit of Truth is the basis of a keener commitment to and an increasing apprehension of the task of Christian theology. The theologian is personally called to follow in the footsteps of him who is the Truth. To do this, he must become totally immersed in the endeavour, holding nothing back. Unconditional commitment to the Word incarnate surpasses limited understanding and theologians experience the abundant life in Christ as the Holy Spirit guides them along the ever-expanding way of Truth.

The sacred and inspired Scriptures record sufficiently all that is required of necessity for Christian theology. The Bible bears witness to the actions of God the Saviour, to the revelation of God, and theologians formulate the doctrines of the Christian faith by reflection on these divine acts. The theologian, however, cannot afford to carry his striving for a systematic theology to the extreme of self-closure. Through the guidance of the Holy Spirit, they achieve open systems that serve him who is the incomparable expression of God the Father.

The meaning of those systems depends on the fidelity with which their conceptual relations accord with the coinherence of the activities of God that centre in the birth, death, resurrection and ascension of Jesus Christ. Without the Holy Spirit such a correspondence cannot be discovered or maintained simply because theological activity engages more than the intellect. The whole person is involved. Passionate devotion is at work rather than neutral abstraction. As theologians submit to the authority of Jesus Christ in their lives, the Spirit of Christ prompts their thinking and doing. Thus, they strive long and hard to find the most appropriate theological utterances that can never be more than indicative in character. Ineffably, the Holy Spirit provides the message and prepares the person to receive it.

A sensitivity to the rationality of the universe is the freedom that scientists develop as they reply positively to the intuitive relation. They proceed in a scientific way, always conscious of the fact that, if they try to possess this freedom, they will lose it, but that, if they are possessed by it, they can travel in the right direction and in good company. In their openness through the intuitive relation, scientists undergo a growing understanding of and a strengthening commitment to this rationality. They move from existing theories describing ranges of phenomena to new theories encompassing even greater, but still limited, domains of experience.[4]

The scientist is called as a person to exercise this freedom. He is recruited as a tracker of truth who puts his whole being into the pursuit. Scientists are inevitably intimately involved in the scientific enterprise. Because their commitment to the rationality of the universe transcends their fragmentary apprehensions, they themselves are changed as the realms of science unfold before them. Einstein's dynamic conception of scientific knowledge is utterly dependent on his postulate of the fundamental intuitiveness of knowledge. The intuitive relation stimulates scientists who travel along person hysteresis loops, experiencing an ever-expanding apprehension of the natural order. Anything written about the intuitive relation, if it is to be authentic, will point to an experience that the scientist cannot thoroughly describe.

The disclosure of the universe is not given in abstractions but in actions. The rationality of the universe presents itself through the intuitive relation as ceaseless series of acts whose number and coordination defy all attempts to quantify or to define them. The intuitive relation guides scientists through the labyrinthine ways of cosmic rationality, enabling the bold intuitions of scientists, as logically free creations of the human mind, to maintain contact with independent reality.[5] Scientific theories are formulated by reflection on the meaning of the actions of the external world. The intuitions of scientists must be tested by the methods and knowledge of contemporary science, by the established theories and practices of scientific research. Their validity is measured by their success in structuring the manifold of observed actions.[6] So far as scientists can understand, their theories and concepts could not have been discovered by reflection apart from the intuitive relation. The plain fact is that new scientific concepts and phenomena are encountered in situations that are never exclusively intellectual.

When scientists are confronted by a new phenomenon or concept, it makes a claim upon them which demands more than intellectual assent. The demand is for a personal response to this novel experience, an involvement that includes the consideration of non-quantitative tokens of reality. Einstein referred to this type of involvement as "a kind of weighing of incommensurable qualities".[7] Contrary to popular non-scientific opinion, scientists cannot dispassionately examine the credentials of a new discovery which makes an authoritative claim upon them. Unavoidably, their immediate scientific statements can only be non-formal in character. Subsequently they search for the appropriate quantitative language in which to express their intuitive appreciation of the importance of their discovery.[8] Mysteriously, the intuitive relation provides the essential condition of effectual scientific intuition, the coincidence of an universal act and a scientific mind prepared to apprehend its meaning.

God is his own Interpreter and, through the Holy Spirit, the biblical record is made plain for all to see. Inspiration, new vision, is accompanied by a command to conform to the Word incarnate and by a confidence in his all-embracing rule of love. Theologians, therefore, are compelled to recognise and to follow what they believe to be the way of Truth and to direct their lives accordingly. Preconceived notions will necessarily obtrude but, given the opportunity, a humble openness to the ministry of the Holy Spirit will eventually triumph. Only the Holy Spirit can preserve and sustain that communion of believers who labour to set aside disreputable ideas derived from purely subjective interpretations. Theologians are inspired by the Holy Spirit to venture honestly and intelligently in faith for Jesus Christ and his Church.

Their labours find expression in theological formulations that are the fruits of extensive and intensive reflection and experience. Because they have had their ears unstopped, they can hear and listen to the Word of God for their day and generation. Their systems represent contributions to the continuous theological dialogue between past and present. Yet, this dialogue is never more than theology in outline. It says more than theologians can hear. Consequently, their progeny hear both what their fathers heard and more. As the Holy Spirit gives them new insights into the richness of the revelation of God in Jesus Christ, the profundities and the inadequacies of older theological systems are more fully appreciated. Each theological generation must experience for itself the reality of the New Covenant in Jesus Christ. To do this, every theologian must steep himself in the ambient theology but not to the neglect of the biblical record of the actions of God the Saviour. Inspired by the Holy Spirit, he can then go on in faith to face new horizons in theological endeavour.

In general terms, scientists humbly acknowledge that, by the courtesy of the universe, their eyes have been opened through the intuitive relation to see the significance of its rationality. This new sight brings with it an obligation to obey that rationality and a sense of security in its comprehensive invariance. Hence, scientists are obliged to accept and to respond favourably to whatever they believe to be meaningful. They must direct their researches not along predetermined lines but as separate reactions to their discoveries. The exposure of falsity and error in science depends on their responses to that obligation. Basically, the intuitive relation disturbs settling scientific thought and rigid scientific routine by prompting the scientific community to press onwards into the unknown. The intuitive relation acts like an acid on all forms of conservatism. Indeed, the intuitive relation holds together a community of scientists each of which, in his individualised personality, pursues bold intuitions that are never certain but that are honestly believed and intelligently investigated.[9]

Scientific theories, however, have mathematical form because they are the products of prolonged deliberation and experimentation by scientific researchers. Since those researchers have seen the light, as it were, they are capable of finding succinct terms for scientific exposition. Their formulations bear the record of scientific progress to future generations. But the things that they seek to express are always greater than they surmise. Thus as science advances, those theories can mediate apprehension in unexpected ways.

All scientists are open through the intuitive relation to the rationality of the universe and so successive generations apprehend both what their predecessors understood and more.[10] Consequently, old theories appear in new contexts with previously unknown interconnections articulated. By the interplay of thought and action, the intuitive relation gives scientists new insights and each scientific generation learns for itself what has been recorded by the original discoverers in science, albeit in a much more condensed form. In every age, scientists must soak themselves in the available scientific knowledge relevant to their particular discipline.[11] Thus imbued, they can tackle scientific research with intuitive faculties finely tuned. They are prepared as far as is humanly possible for those experiences when, through the initiative of the intuitive relation, the solution to a problem appears on the conceptual horizon.

Such an experience is not a chaotic irruption or a haphazard intervention. The years of scientific training enriched by subsequent research together with continued study of the recent literature of his discipline and stimulating discussions with colleagues, all of these exercise his intuitive abilities. They help to equip him to receive illumination in unfamiliar situations. Bluntly, what appears to the non-scientist to be conceptual bolts from the blue are instances of the initiative of the intuitive relation carrying the responsive scientist beyond what was antecedently apprehended. The scientist is equal to the novel and unprecedented situation because he can rely upon this relation to raise him to meet the scientific emergency. The intuitive relation promotes the growth of scientific wisdom and freedom.

Apparently, the role of the intuitive relation in science is like a faint echo of the work of the Holy Spirit in theology. Once again, the similarity is restricted by the absence of an inter-personal bond between the intuitive relation and the scientist. Clearly, the indwelling Holy Spirit is the divine Person who ministers to persons. Still, a remarkable correspondence becomes evident when science is viewed from an Einsteinian standpoint. This particular congruity represents one more facet of an extensive correlation of scientific research and theological activity, a correspondence which strongly suggests that modern science and modern theology have considerable common origins. On those foundations it may be possible to build a new bridge between science and theology that will serve the interests of both.

NOTES

1. *Ideas and Opinions*, pp. 261f.
2. *Philosopher-Scientist*, pp. 15f.
3. *Later Years*, p. 61.
4. *Scientific Revolutions*, p. 3.
5. *Ideas and Opinions*, p. 271. See also V. F. Lenzen, *Philosopher-Scientist*, p. 361.
6. *Later Years*, p. 60.
7. *Philosopher-Scientist*, p. 21. See also *A Centenary Volume*, pp. 265f and *Thematic Origins*, pp. 219–259.
8. *Ideas and Opinions*, pp. 25f.
9. *Later Years*, p. 60.
10. *Ideas and Opinions*, p. 271. See also V. F. Lenzen, *Philosopher-Scientist*, p. 361.
11. *Later Years*, p. 64.

Chapter 10

MOTIVATION AND COMMUNITY

FROM an Einsteinian perspective, an extensive correspondence between modern science and Christian theology comes readily to light. Einstein, however, was firmly convinced that, although "a cosmic religious feeling is the strongest and noblest motive for scientific research",[1] this feeling "can give rise to no definite notion of God and no theology".[2] Science does not lead to God but it does not exclude him. Einstein never lost sight of the reality that the scientist working with a limited range of sense impressions could not give a complete account of the world he was investigating. Certainly, the scientist can answer with considerable confidence some of the questions put to him, but he can make no legitimate pronouncements on those aspects of reality which he has not researched, never intended to research, and has no means of researching.

Obviously, Einstein was well aware of the quasi-religious nature of science but he also saw the need in science to avoid all pretensions of the transcendental. According to him, "science without religion is lame, religion without science is blind".[3] While conceding that science has a religious basis and that religion includes scientific vision, he refused to equate the roles of the scientist and the theologian. He referred to the correspondence as "a conviction, akin to religious feeling, of the rationality or intelligibility of the world (which) lies behind all scientific work of a higher order".[4] And the more one considers such comments the more one appreciates the great wisdom which gave them utterance. Curiously, while science has attained a measure of popularity the Spirit which motivates its activities is seldom acknowledged.

Certainly, modern science should be treated with respect by theologians for, as Einstein sensed, it can raise old theological questions in new contexts.[5] It would appear, for example, that intuition is to theory in science what revelation is to doctrine in theology. Sometimes, intuitions visit scientists like revelations. Einstein's experience had led him to believe in a God who could give the scientist "a sense of the ultimate and fundamental ends. To make clear these fundamental ends and valuations, and to set them fast in the emotional life of the individual, seems to me precisely the most important function which religion has to perform in the social life of men."[6] Those ends "came into being not through demonstration but through revelation, through the medium of powerful personalities. One must not attempt to justify them, but rather to sense their nature simply and clearly."[7] Could it be that revelation is actually a human problem and not a distinctively theological question?

Hope and faith are kindled by scientific research. Every scientist looks to the future. Scientific research is beginning what others will enjoy and develop. The actions of scientists, not the practical results of science, maintain the scientific enterprise. Free inquiry and personal activity characterise modern science. To be creative in science, the person must be prepared to spend himself for the sake of those who follow. The combination of unqualified generosity and uncompromising criticism is so efficacious in scientific research precisely because it reflects the uniqueness of the rationality of the universe. This rationality gives freely, orders invariantly and invites activities in kind from scientific researchers. Consequently, scientists regard modern science not merely as one response among others to the structured universe but *the* valid reaction to the physical world.

The way of life offered by science fires conviction and enthusiasm, and it seems to many people to be more open and appealing than that of Christianity. For example, when Galileo investigated the law governing the motion of falling bodies, he cared passionately about discovering that law but he remained open-minded about the exact nature of the law. Similarly, Newton's law of inverse squares and

Einstein's general theory of relativity appealed to open scientific minds and fired the enthusiasm of committed scientific researchers. The details of the discoveries of science are a matter of relative indifference until their heuristic connectivities begin to be appreciated.

Couldn't theologians learn something from the candour of scientists about their uncertainties despite the depths of their convictions? The scientific enterprise does not promise to provide answers to all the questions, demands and miseries of mankind. But, because it can supply the means by which to attain such ends, it enjoys considerable prestige.[8] Perhaps, if the Church were more outspoken about the creative role of theology and less critical of the pedagogic value of theology, it could become more convincing about the reality that theology is never a substitute for Jesus Christ who is the only answer to all men's needs. Too often the Churches guard ill-chosen ground and defend untenable constructions.

Scientific researchers should, in their turn, respect Christian theology for, as Einstein acknowledged, religion provides the basic motivation for science. He realised that "science, in the immediate, produces knowledge, and, indirectly, means of action. It leads to methodical action if definite goals are set up in advance. For the function of settling up goals and passing statements of value transcends its domain."[9] It is, perhaps, only those who have lived in the midst of modern science and theological activity for a while who can realise in how deep a sense the latter has shaped the background and the unconsciously accepted principles of the former, though the number of scientific researchers who are also devoted Christians may be relatively few. There are many scientists of sound realism and commitment who never read Christian theology and consider themselves agnostics but as a matter of history owe much to theology. In reality, they are living on borrowed capital.

It was observed earlier that the rationality of the universe is essentially inclusive and not primarily exclusive. This rationality is not exclusive in the sense that all other forms of knowledge are rendered invalid. Whatever is found to be valid in non-scientific systems of knowledge is often included and expanded by modern science. Indeed, Einstein believed that scientific thought is a refinement of everyday thinking.[10] The relation of ancient Greek thought to modern science supports his assertion. Characteristically, the first philosophers of ancient Greece searched for a "material cause" of all things. As the world consists of matter, a natural point of departure in such a search was the identification of the "material cause" with water. This Thales did, but Heraclitus chose fire. Such identifications with existing forms of matter led on to speculation about the smallest parts of matter and to the hypothesis of the "atom" or the indivisible unit of matter.

Leucippus and Democritus were the founders of atomism. They first stated that the "atom" is eternal and indestructible, and that all other things exist only because they are composed of "atoms". The empty space between them allows for their motions, accounts for the properties of "atoms", and the different states of matter can be explained, an attribute of the atomic hypothesis that has been successfully included in modern science. However, the "atoms" turn out to be molecules that are neither eternal nor indivisible. Such concepts are transcended in modern atomic theory. Nevertheless, the atomic hypothesis of the ancient Greek philosophers carried modern scientists a long way toward current apprehension.

Concepts are modified and reformulated as scientific horizons appear. Yet the expansion of apprehension in its distinctly scientific form is not merely a claim that predictions can be verified. Rather it is the inclusive affirmation of the rationality of the universe as the invariant foundation of modern science. This belief is the reverse of exclusiveness and lies behind all scientific research with its fragmented rationalities. What scientific eyes see, scientific ears hear, and scientific hands handle is the rationality of the universe as an inclusiveness that involves all that may be described as scientific.

This means that scientists can and do learn from philosophers, theologians and artists. While they believe that all knowledge of the physical world is included in the rationality of the universe, there is still much to be gleaned from non-scientific sources of knowledge. Yet modern science does not syncretise that knowledge. Scientists seek the roots of all concepts in the soil of experimental science. Consequently, the study of other forms of knowledge becomes relevant to science only in so far as it fires the intuition of the scientist who believes that all knowledge of the physical world rationally belongs to the universe. In fact, scientists are prevented from rejecting this extraordinary claim by scientific research, which convinces them that it is justified. But, in the absence of personal experience, it is difficult for non-scientists to appreciate the meaning and validity of that claim.

The depth and relevance of Einstein's insights are indicated but not exhausted by the preceding sections of this essay. Of course, mere coincidence of views is no proof of influence but the extent and context of the coincidence of scientific and theological thought can imply influence. Unquestionably, science owes a great deal to Christian theology, a debt that has been largely ignored and grossly underestimated until relatively recently. There is still much work to be done before the historical accounts are properly balanced. Christianity, in spite of its checkered past, provided, for example, the paradigms for intellectual freedom, integrity and humility in modern science. And science's history has reinforced the Christian lessons that persons cannot accept knowledge solely on the authority of someone else nor assume that there is no understanding except by their own limited reflections. Christianity taught science the value of tradition and unfortunately demonstrated many of its abuses. In the authority of Jesus Christ, it also paved the way for the authority of the rational universe and it proclaimed that real authority is not dictatorial but relates to personal insight. Consequently, scientists as individuals depend on ears open to both the harmony of nature and the voices of their fellow researchers.

From the very beginnings of modern science, researchers were not restricted to their own small experience. They assimilated freely what others claimed before them as they themselves apprehended those claims. Copernicus, for instance, built his heliocentric system upon the Ptolemaic system. Like Kepler, Galileo and all the other fathers of science, Copernicus was indebted to many previous pathfinders. In this important respect, modern scientists are not any different. Even Einstein owed much to Newton. Bluntly, a scientist is not worth his salt if he neglects the accumulated wisdom of the centuries. Indeed, science is progressive in the sense that more and more is discovered and every scientific researcher builds on the achievements of his predecessors.[11] In science, as in theology, integrity must be clothed in humility. Obedience is the order of the scientific day and that demands a profound sense of humility. The scientist is free to choose to obey his intuition in order to convert it into scientific theory. He is free to decide to listen humbly to whoever can advance his thinking and doing. Hence, the scientific researcher learns whenever and wherever he can. Scientific research mixes as well with pride as oil does with water.

Nevertheless, there is a great temptation to overestimate the logical nature of science, a trend that could be partially reversed by informed theologians. Mathematics alone does not sustain the scientific endeavour. In fact, the contrary can sometimes occur. For centuries, Euclidean geometry reigned supreme in science as if by divine right until the advent and application of non-Euclidean geometries expanded scientific horizons. Characteristically, the salient point was made by Einstein. "As far as propositions of mathematics refer to reality, they are not certain, and as far as they are certain, they do not refer to reality".[12] Einstein knew that the intuitions of scientists baffle the ranges of words and mathematics. In those intuitive moments, there is, no doubt, a logical element but it is inadequate and secondary. Mathematics or logic becomes predominant only when the door to analysis and reporting is opened.

A scientific theory is more or less an agreed statement of the scientific community. This logically free imperfect creation is an attempt to express what it means to glimpse the wonder of the universe in terms of its own rationality. But the truth-content of a theory is not the same thing as the intuition of the scientist. The former only points to the latter. A scientific theory is ineffective and misleading in so far as it diverts attention away from that intuition. Scientific theories are more than persuasive mathematical expositions. They touch an intuitive nerve as they inject a sense of wonder evoking a response which involves the mind, will and being of the scientist. In other words, science deals with concepts that always break through mathematics and escape comprehension. This does not diminish, however, scientific faith which rests in the universe, not in the theories of science.

In so many respects, therefore, theological concepts are like their scientific counterparts. Logic is not the exclusive basis of theology. Logical investigation cannot reveal the connections between theological concepts and Christian experience. The moment of revelation defies comprehensive articulation. Christian doctrines are agreed statements of the Churches that try to convey something of what it means to experience the miracle of the Word incarnate in terms of his Rationality. Those doctrines are not the same as the revelation of God to man. They are only signs along the way. Theology involves concepts that burst out of logic and elude definition. They do not thereby threaten Christian faith which is anchored in the eternal Word of God, not in transient theological formulations. Clearly, the theologian is well equipped to converse with and encourage the scientist and to maintain a healthy regard for logic and mathematics.

By recognising the discursive, topological and heuristic qualities of scientific thinking, theologians and scientists, alike, can prepare themselves for the constructive discovery that they already share much more than they realise. For example, both systematic theology and scientific research presuppose the surmounting of difficulties and their statements are not meaningless even if they cannot be reduced without remainder to prosaic definition. Consequently, where there is a variance between science and theology, it should not lead to the rash abandonment of theories or doctrines for which there are substantial empirical grounds. To remain faithful to both science and theology, a deeper appreciation of theory and doctrine should be earnestly pursued. In its absence, speculation should be avoided because it will only frustrate the attainment of the reconciliation of a more mature theology and a more rational science. To attempt to unravel every entanglement of thought is to minimise the destruction of candour, to maximise the openness of inquiry and to counteract the stagnation of orthodoxy.

Because the universe is invariant, its disclosures to scientists are the same for it is the one and only universe that self-discloses. Because God is unoriginate, his revelation to all persons is the one Lord Jesus Christ. Yet, scientists, theologians and generations are different. Insight varies from person to person. Consequently, intuition or inspiration leads to different scientific or theological expositions whose common terms point to the same reality. At best, science or theology can only ever begin to understand reality. Of necessity, scientists or theologians remain in awe of the immeasurable mastery that enfolds the world and human life. They all experience a sense of wonder as they explore the whole of which they are but tiny fragments. In fact, it is questionable whether any scientist or theologian can really believe in the rationality of the universe or the Person of Jesus Christ unless they have personally experienced how inconceivable and incredible life really is.

Like the Church, the scientific community is an assembly of believers. Its members participate of their own free will in the mystery of the harmony of the universe. They exchange honestly scientific knowledge and they teach sincerely their theories. The same can be said of theologians and their doctrines. The meaning of this universal scientific association resides in its cooperation with the rationality of the universe as communicated by its theories and experiments. Compare it with the reality of the Church which is its participation in the work and word of Jesus Christ by worship and mission. This scientific community mediates its involvement in the natural order and in the freedom deriving from it, just as the Church witnesses to its Lord and its God-given liberty. The centre of scientific gravity lies in its identity as the assembly of all believers of which the personal freedom of the scientist is the basis and strength. Christian freedom plays a similar role in the Church. Scientists associate with one another, sooner or later, because they belong inalienably together through the intuitive relation and they communicate either by direct contact or by means of the scientific literature. Likewise, Christians are indissolubly united the world over by the one Holy Spirit and they interrelate personally or by means of the Christian literature. Evidently, the natures of the scientific community and of the Church display some common features.

The scientific community is the sphere of activity of the intuitive relation which emanates from the external world and its rationality, and which propagates to all scientists. Correspondingly, the Church is the province of the ministry of the Holy Spirit who proceeds from the Father and the Son and who inspires all believers. While scientists believe in the rationality of the universe, they also acknowledge the existence of this scientific fraternity which conducts its business in relative isolation from the non-scientific world. Of course, like theologians, scientists come together as persons with all sorts of conflicting prejudices, passions and insights. Free and candid interchange of thought, a pooling of all their resources, criticisms and convictions, binds them into a community of common endeavour. But neither scientists nor theologians are turned out with mechanical uniformity like the products of the lathe, rather they find themselves with that freedom which derives from a community of persons. In both science and theology, apprehension is a corporate process.

To be a member of the Church or of the scientific community is not to be made perfect. The Holy Spirit or the intuitive relation enlivens the latent energies in the person. Always, there are novel possibilities of manipulation as well as of legitimate investigation. Ambitions are evoked and powers are released which have to be controlled or resisted. The histories of the Church and modern science are not without the stains and strains of stagnation, strife and sedition. Nevertheless, those communities have enriched human life. In spite of its frailties and deficiencies, the scientific fraternity belongs to the universe and, therefore, to all mankind in the sense that it adds to the quality of human life. Similarly, the Church is in the world, for the world but not of the world.

The separateness of this community, reminiscent of the holiness of the Church, demands unconditionally the unity of all scientists. But unity is not uniformity either in the Church or in the scientific community. There is always room for honest disagreement in science as in theology. Disputes do not obscure the underlying unity of all scientific researchers or of all Christian proclamation. Instead, by highlighting areas that have been inadequately apprehended or investigated, those disagreements focus attention on the supreme rationality of the universe or the unique revelation of God in Jesus Christ.

As already indicated, the scientific community or the Church numbers only a part of mankind among its members. The business of the Church or of the scientific community lifts its members beyond the bounds of nation, culture or sex. The universality of these communities is closely linked with their unities. Both depend on the progressive modes of thought developed and communicated throughout many generations. They maintain their continuities because their members pursue personally and relentlessly the appropriate way. As the privileges of minorities, these pursuits must dominate every aspect of the life of the community. In other words, the separateness, unity, universality and continuity of the scientific community are as intimately connected as are the holiness, unity, catholicity and apostolicity of the Church. Indeed, these attributes can be regarded as the criteria of the great human adventures embarked on by the assemblies of believers in the rationality of the universe and in the Lord Jesus Christ. Obviously, the marks of science echo to some extent the marks of the Church.

Nevertheless, there are significant differences between the scientific community and the Church but they can be better appreciated in the light of their resemblances. From the preceding sections of this essay, it is fairly evident that modern science offers the scientist a vocation, a calling to serve "in the temple of science".[13] This involves a faith that, in many ways, seems to match the Christian faith. Indeed, scientific faith appears to be an intensely intellectual, individualised, solitary variant of Christian faith. Dealing with the non-moral universal order, it encourages scientists to develop an interest in things as opposed to persons.

Scientific thinking requires freedom from humanitarian motivations. Scientific optimisn sees an increasing apprehension of the universe as an enrichment of the quality of human life. Scientists are trained for research, not dissemination. According to Einstein, most of them are "somewhat odd, uncommunicative solitary fellows, really less like each other in spite of common characteristics, than the hosts of the rejected".[14] Few of them do not appreciate that it is better to destroy privately one's own illusions than to be publicly discredited by one's colleagues. The personal gifts of scientists are obscured by the emphasis on objective reporting in the scientific literature. The short range interests of many scientists who are successful researchers completely saturate their capabilities for forming long-range connections.[15] While science is valued by laymen mainly for its practical applications, the latter tend to be regarded by scientists as the by-products of the scientific enterprise.

Still, science provides the means for both a vital mechanism for cultural change and an aid to an apprehension of that change.[16] Consequently, modern science has found itself misunderstood in many parts of the world as a remarkable rival spiritual movement to Christianity. For many disillusioned minds, it represents a passionate idealism which speaks of a new order of society without privilege of birth, wealth, or greed. It anticipates that poverty, hunger and illness shall no longer afflict the common man. According to many, modern science can offer human beings a guide to the conduct of their lives. For them, it prescribes a system of conduct which has for its basis participation in the way of the universe, as interpreted from its self-disclosures and the scientific knowledge of humankind who are cells in the cosmic corpus. Yet, as Einstein indicated, there is no direct connection between these hopes and ideals on the one side and modern science on the other. In reality, they are incompatibles. The fiction of dominant science providing the only intellectually acceptable view of the world is more the product of the non-scientific imagination than the conviction of the scientific researcher. It is tragic for both modern science and Christian theology, and for mankind as a whole, that the much needed hope for civilisation should be linked with superficial materialism.

The theologian must not dismiss too lightly, however, such interpretations of the scientific enterprise. Having so much in common, modern science could reasonably be described as Christian theology operating in a different gear. Exacting personal commitment, learning and experience characterise scientific research. And scientists will need more than a logical refutation to convince them of the futility of some of their hopes for the unpredictable future, particularly when those hopes are already externally motivated. Equally, scientists should be more open to the commitment, learning and experience of theologians whose forebears seem to have set the stage for the enthralling performances of modern science. The urgent call is for honest dialogue based on extensive personal participation, that is, founded on both Christian and scientific realism.

Perhaps, the preceding sketches of the similarities between scientific and Christian faith, scientific and theological communication, scientific and Christian knowledge, the universe and God, the rationality of the universe and the Lord Jesus Christ, the intuitive relation and the Holy Spirit, and the scientific community and the Church will encourage others of greater insight to contribute to the exciting, promising and reconciling dialogue which is still in its infancy. At minimum, they suggest that science and theology are not independent disciplines, that each discipline should not reject the other, that theology is no more a form of superstition than science is a species of heresy, and that the metaphysical aspects of science hold out the promise of an increased interface of science and theology. They also point to the powerful significance of Einstein's thoughts on modern science.

Through scientific wisdom, which appears to be a daughter of Christian wisdom, there lies the possibility of a better life on this planet. Science itself, however, does not motivate the determination that there shall be a new world order. As Einstein said, this motivation must come from another source.[17] Generally, it springs from the Christian background and, therefore, specifically from Jesus Christ. While every scientist recognises that the purpose of the universe must lie beyond the universe itself, if it has a purpose, and that some day human history will disappear in the cosmic flux, he is motivated by the desire to apprehend, the need to believe and the will to search. He places his hope in the rationality of the universe which he can only see dimly, the same rationality which begins and ends in the Person of the Lord Jesus Christ.

NOTES

1. *Ideas and Opinions*, p. 39.
2. *Ibid.*, p. 38.
3. *Ibid.*, p. 55.
4. *Ibid.*, p. 262.
5. A. Einstein, *The World As I See It*, translated by A. Harris, New York: Citadel Press, 1979, pp. 111f.
6. *Ideas and Opinions*, pp. 42f.
7. *Ibid.*

8. *Later Years*, p. 124.
9. *Ideas and Opinions*, p. 50.
10. *Later Years*, p. 59.
11. *Ideas and Opinions*, p. 271. See also V. F. Lenzen, *Philosopher-Scientist*, p. 361.
12. *Ideas and Opinions*, p. 233.
13. *Ibid.*, p. 224.
14. *Ibid.*, pp. 225f.
15. *Thematic Origins*, p. 463.
16. *Ibid.*, p. 462.
17. *Ideas and Opinions*, p. 42.